©2021 by Beaudelaine Pierre
First Edition
Library of Congress Control Number: 2019956999
ISBN: 978-0-89823-399-5
e-ISBN: 978-0-89823-400-8

New Rivers Press is a nonprofit literary press associated with Minnesota State University Moorhead.

Cover design by Tara Kennedy
Interior design by Nayt Rundquist
Author photo by Annie Faith
Interior Images: Johannah Hallin and Annie Faith

The publication of *You May Have the Suitcase Now* is made possible by the generous support of Minnesota State University Moorhead, the Dawson Family Endowment, and other contributors to New Rivers Press.

MINNESOTA STATE UNIVERSITY MOORHEAD.

This publication is funded in part by a grant from the Lake Region Arts Council through a Minnesota State Legislative appropriation.

Lake Region Arts Council

NRP Staff: Nayt Rundquist, Managing Editor; Kevin Carollo, Editor; Travis Dolence, Director; Trista Conzemius, Art Director
Interns: Gabbie Brandt, Dana Casey, Alex Ferguson, Shaina Garman, Alise Ilkka, Katie Martinson, Geneva Nodland, Delaney Noe, Andrew Reed, Olivia Rockstad

You May Have the Suitcase Now book team: Madisen Anderson, Gaëtan Hartmann, Samuel Schroeder

Printed in the USA on acid-free, archival-grade paper.

You May Have the Suitcase Now is distributed nationally by Small Press Distribution.

New Rivers Press
c/o MSUM
1104 7th Ave S
Moorhead, MN 56563
www.newriverspress.com

To my parents,

Mariette Belhomme and Louis St-Juste Necker Pierre

Nou te konn tande grandèt yo, e nou fè eksperyans lan;
fè timoun yo konnen ki kote yo soti.
—Marie Lily Cérat

Voici mon secret. Il est très simple:
on ne voit bien qu'avec le cœur.
L'essentiel est invisible pour les yeux.
—Antoine de Saint-Exupéry

What you see on the page is only part of the story.
—Olive Senior

Contents

-1-
The Kids and the Big Issues

Freedom

They are singing in the back seat of the car as we drive through Marshall Ave. Nobody choruses like them. A spectacle of tunes stifled and sifted through a sieve of yells, screams, and clatter the Oxford English Dictionary will not bother to confer with. But I may need to find out what this release is about far away from the seashore of confederate categories of legitimate enjoyments.

Behind the wheels I picture uvula, epiglottis, pharynx, larynx, tongues, and tunes spilled out and piling up on the car's carpet. They are dancing too; against their cumbersome belts. The windows are down. They slide forte falsetto from "Treat You Better" to "Uptown Funk" and whatever else the radio in the car is giving away freely, freely.

The kids are raw. They jangle in their seats like damp leaves mounted on the back of angry clouds who just got poked at. And the car goes in staccato. And I am now an expired audience whose taste can't be trusted anymore. Towards the outside they swerve, throw their organs away. Other drivers and passersby must not miss the flow. And the kids explode, shrill, and sing as loudly as they can with "Diamonds" or "Just Give Me a Reason," like they weren't asking anyone's permission to charge freedom.

What else do I need? There are no reasons not to stifle freedom bubbles in the open air like water you sprinkle out in brilliant streaks you assume won't come back to you. No one has yet declared ownership of the open air. But too much happiness leads the lamb to the butchery. I will have to refrain their energy. I restrain my enjoyment. The gentleman crossing the street right before us has his fingers suddenly clutched in a fist. Just last week a driver pulled the trigger on another driver driving before him. The other driver was driving too slowly, too happily too, I suppose. Children screaming, shouting, singing, and feeling what they feel are no good signs. I pull up all the car windows, ask the kids to calm down. They scream, they shout, they sing we live in a free country! And Before I realize, Spangled Banner has become Strangled Banner.

I calm myself down. The new era is on parade, unflinching; and the old, so unintimidated. Truth is, freedom is the saccharine you receive on your tongue in small sifting doses. Definitely not the appropriate moment for an allied definition of bondage in the Youwès, I mean freedom, well, forget it. "Cheap Thrills."

Ramsey vs TCA

It will be TCA. My daughter wishes for Ramsey. In the small of her back like a permanent ghost, the schoolmaster with basic training in population control. Her friends from her elementary school will start middle school at Ramsey. A few friends of mine, African born and raised, advise for TCA. One never thought of keeping a record of things the way one counts the dead as if moved by survivor's guilt. But you notice Erica Garner departing a few years after Eric Garner; a five-year-old boy staggering when he sees the police or buying Nerf and darts and guns with each Target gift card; he dreams of being a policeman and this isn't enough to put him on the side of the survivors. His second-grade reading level will advise the government on new measures against felons, pardon, black cons. You slowly begin to contemplate what you ought not to see in the cycle of things unfailingly repeating themselves. I am being a bit historical, here.

With some of that in the small of my back, I show up one morning for a surprise visit to Ramsey. The building is silent, heavily secured, and the staff friendly, wanting, and waiting. They have time for an unannounced visitor, no kidding. I do not mean to keep track of things. Besides, in the entanglement of who does what to whom, I may as well be the object upon which calculations and tracks are tallied. Survivors are not inclined to see themselves tallied upon. And guilt sometimes is oblivion, sometimes judgement, and other times, innocence. I exchange emails and phone numbers with one of the state counselors. The kinds who are trained to instruct me on how my people group is good at nursing, at carpentering, and taxi-driving if they are lucky enough to avoid the prison ceiling. The point is that I do not keep score. Inseparable from that terror, you wait for the name of the next pupil to align with the Garners. You also notice that surviving is slowly dying with a bit of hysteria inside.

The state counselor and I will talk over the phone to set up an appointment. In my agenda we will talk about how a good school is not good for all its children. The school counselor is a black woman. I will tell her black to black and woman to woman you can't fool me, tell me the truth. I will talk about differential expectations, flawed preconceptions, misbehaved status quo, and made-up minorities. A song the state counselor already knows. We will sit face to face. I will empty my gut and continue telling her things she knows, like the story of another state agent who told one of her pupils they should not dream too high. This is not even the problem. The state counselor knows the real problem the way I know of a school mistress in another establishment who told a minority student they are not fit for colleges and universities. The state counselor I am meeting with will say, we are different, we are better, I will agree. And I will continue telling her things she already knows and talking and not listening. I am already defeated, distorted, and in the wrong. I bet she calls her pupils who are of my daughter's tribe, minorities. But this, I won't tell her, that no survivior is a minority, their numbers are too expansive, see what I mean? I have a suspicion: the school counselor is a survivor.

I am leaving the facility. The camp is clean, the staff safely unguarded, the high torture chamber, dramatic. And you enhance the solemnity of the moment by marching with your two footed body on the ground and holding your shoulders up high, like the steadfast soldier with a rested prisoner inside. I find my way in between large walls made up of steel and bricks, in between high doors with small windows at the top and from which students are to be observed. I feel highly secure. The state counselor owes allegiance to Ramsey no matter how much she already knows. She will not throw in the towel for a pretentious stranger who seems to have been to the prison system herself and have survived it with guilt, blame, and oblivion, but not with innocence.

I leave the Bastille for good. At home I throw at my daughter, that I am deliberating upon it. Ramsey vs TCA. I will not call the state counselor. I will not sit with her to be told things I already know. I will not tell her about things she already knows. Between the two of us, I can only imagine all the noise and the imagined communities putting to sleep so many things to account for, like the school counselor in derangement with the state. Anyway, TCA, this is it. And I still don't know in what way this inclination makes things any better for my daughter.

Fast but slow

They cross the street fast. Go to the grocery store fast. They crunch fast the potato chips they cart fast from the grocery store. They run a walk. They work their reading compositions fast and have a blast over the words and the sentences they fast. They race the rain, walk home swift and fast, and take the stairs fast to fall asleep steadfast in their wet clothes drying fast. They swab the living room fast, wash the dishes fast, and swallow fast in half-clean plates their meals and their left-over crap. They hop in the car fast, buckle up fast, and ask very fast about the fastest race I've ever fastened. And in between your teeth you connect very fast: a McDonald Big mac + Beware bipeds and pets at play + An elected president who reads as slow as molasses. They talk and dance and write and move like winds rolling and breaking things swift and tight. They say I am slow I drive slow I read slow I talk slow. The only thing I am fast at is eating and drinking they say of the way I eat fast while standing and running and fasting. They are right that I would also miss the click in the photo shoot that goes too fast, then too slow. I am a slow walker, a slow thinker, a slow learner, and enjoy being just that, a sloth. I wonder now very fast where I had gotten the idea that slowness is the proper way to go. And doing it all over again in slow motion, I would fast the line about the commander-in-chief who is, now that you think of all the preceding, believably slow.

On 8 hours

I have never given serious thought about my children or myself having ADHD or Asperger's syndrome or other expected accepted orderings. In the Youwès, some bodies are normal, others are reordered unproductive. A normal body stands up for 8 hours or more each day to produce goods, then go home in the evening to drive their family to the shopping mall where they pay for the TV or the latest pillow or the new electronic gadgets, the gods, the goods they have assembled and put into packages days or weeks or months before. After the trip to the shopping mall, the normal body is summoned, go home, sit down, and watch TV restfully for three hours or more. They put together the TV, too. After watching the news, the ordered body, asleep but accommodating and cooperative, goes back to work for another night shift then returns home to catch a few hours of sleep if they can. Afterwards, they wake up the day after, well the same day, you're right, to produce the same ritual, the same plot, the same device: their bodies who manufacture themselves nights and days, asleep but productive and profitable. It's true your TV box is made in Sendomeng and you produce free-to-air services behind your screen from your bedroom. The gods indeed are creative and powerful. More than ever you are busy, occupied, and rented, mind, body, and soul, ubering, lyfting, and amazoning all the while you're crying, bring back American jobs. In the grammar of the body Made in U.S.A., my children and myself suffer autism syndrome, hostility syndrome, apathy syndrome, trump syndrome, and all the dromes you can think of. We cannot stand up on our two feet for eight hours to produce goods seven days a week. We cannot think straight, sit straight, talk straight. Our bodies will not walk to the MOA and to all the other shopping malls, nor sit our derrieres to watch the news or Dr. Phil for four hours straight. Or is it, as my son said once, "*you have no money?*" Anyway, our bodies are unaccommodating, disobliging, unproductive. And despite being disease-inflicted, we won't bring our disorderly bodies to the doctor.

Private property
My son is travelling his hands on the neighborhood houses' walls as we walk on the sidewalk. But then, the walls are so neat, the houses so carefully equally metered, and the neighbor so watchfully on their lawn; you can't imagine yourself out of line. I freak

out, I yell don't touch it's not your house. Yet, it isn't easy to walk through a day of to-do-lists, of bills, of shifts, and lottery dreams without a vision of the neighborhood and its walls and us within them, free, unbounded, infinite, and mixed into each other. I am mad, I'm angry, what's wrong with me? How to explain to a four-year-old he cannot touch a wall? It's true that not walking on the neighbor's grass, not touching their walls, not parking in front of their alley, or not looking at them straight in the eyes might just save my son's life. The rule of personal space, of body control, of copyright, and pick-up-after-yourself. Shame on me for teaching a toddler about

   pri-pri-pri-pri-pri-private property. Somebody better call the spirits.

Being a mom

My seven-year-old daughter is already throwing here and there
when I become a mom I will do this I will do that.
I sigh I shrink I moan
Then there was the day when my nine-year-old daughter said
I will befriend my kids and we'
ll drive through life with a low mileage of yells, of spanks, and black beans
hmf hmmf hmmph
and at twelve-year-old my daughters says
I am going to name them Poem, Haiku, and Rhapsody
In the matter of things falling apart I now feel like screaming and yelling
who taught you that becoming a mom is a *passage obligé*?
Then I relax.
why in the hell am I making such a fuss about my seven-year-old daughter wanting to be me
another me I mean.

Race

My third grader arrives at home after her first day at school:
I have met my teacher today, he's very cool, and smart.
My first-grade son is, too, on his first day
What's the race of your teacher?
I like my teacher too, he's from Togo and speaks French.

And my daughter shivers
I am not going to tell you, why does this matter?
The following day the brother was at it again,
what is the race of your teacher?
An air of outspoken hunger
one teacher between them
no, two, or
something else on parade getting in the way:
an impossible change.
I am not going to tell anyone about it, it does not matter whether he's brown or blue or pink.
I agree with my daughter, and the following year I asked the school to place my kids with teachers from Togo.

Ramblings

She said she does not know how she got from here to there We were doing this activity in the gym she said and I decided to take a break and one of the coaches came to me asked me for my name where I go to school if I have siblings I told the coach I plan to go to TCA next year I will take French at TCA instead of Spanish that I was at French Immersion last year and the coach asked me if I know people who speak French I say yes my mom and my little brother speak French we arrived here from Haiti two weeks before the earthquake to visit my mom who was going to school at the University of Minnesota and I told the coach Max was born in New York and the coach asked me how old I was when I came here I was three or four or something I said I cannot quite remember and the coach said that's an incredible story As I listen to my daughter's chatter I nod the coach is right she really knows how to tell a story and before I could say anything my daughter quickly jumps and carries on I do not know how I got from talking about taking a break while at the gym to telling the whole story of my family arriving here from Haiti sometimes I talk too much I ramble I annoy people don't you think and I do not know how to stop and I talk I talk the way I talk to you now But now I truly need to take a break, by the way whenever I speak with you will you let me know if I annoy you I will let you know I said and the day after after pondering over talking or not talking over talking less or more and over rambling I came to my daughter told her you get to talk as much as you can my girl talk talk talk talk very loud you get winds and ramble as you please Make noise too every time you feel like noisying and do not bother asking yourself whether you annoy people when they threaten to grab you by you-know-what and move on you as they please A flood from which I also quickly pull myself.

Christopher Columbus

My nine-year-old daughter comes to me pissed off, in tears, and angry. *What's wrong? Max called me Christopher Columbus.* Then Max comes up, *she threatened to destroy the Minecraft village I built.* He's also pissed and angry. The two share an iPad and my son's passion this year is to build houses, open bank accounts, and decide if he should buy the Lamborghini or the Bugatti. "Have you seen a Bugatti?" he asks me the other day. He has and he knows the brands of all possible car brands and drives one or two in his Minecraft and Roblox universe. Then, I am suddenly taken from my reveries with my daughter screaming, *I am not Christopher Columbus, I am not a murderer or a serial killer, it's like you're saying I destroyed the Native of Ayiti.* The brother knew the right button to push; this is noteworthy. I can now move on to the next.

Brother, I Am Dying

In L'Énigme Du Retour, Dany Laferriere writes about the anxiety of the Haitian immigrant. Something I presumed was mine alone to deal with, and I kept it buried under an American air suffused with Burger kings, corn syrups, and tornado shifts. But since reading about what I knew but wouldn't assert, I have become a little comfortable with my terror of death on alien land. In this anxiety you imagine yourself alive no matter how dead you already are, and the faraways quickly disappearing.

So, usually, when I receive a call from Haiti, my heartbeats speed up: who else is sick? What else is going on? Has something bad happened? Often the call is a typical check-in and my heart condition is stabilized for a few more weeks. When more than two weeks have passed and I do not receive a call, to finally watch the 509-number racing and dancing on my cellphone screen is enough to give me a panic attack. My chest grows tight, my heartbeat overdoes it, and I imagine the worst in moderate over-exaggeration. In truth I am the one dying.

My parents will live to be one hundred or almost. I won't. My grandma passed at ninety-eight. The minutes right before she crossed, her body walked up the ground in equal proportion to the big passage, defiant, and alive forever. So, in Haiti I pictured I would carry on healthily, happily, joyfully at one hundred. Nowadays. I go to bed. I ask myself. Will I wake up the next morning? Nowadays I live in the Youwèsey, it's been almost a decade, and my body dead and dying.

We were in the fall of 2016. We lived in a carrel on Marshall Ave, and we spent our entire days on the edge of the Mississippi river to escape the shit smell of our cells, and we filled our stomachs with bleached bread for illusion of fulfillments. The streets around us were in migration overflowed with laughs, large bellies, and fireworks blazed the air as if they were making a statement. We all knew the emptiness there is.

Every day now, on the top of my innerspring sofa made of unearthed anxiety and terror, I ruminate over the kind of troubles the kids will inherit. I have no proper will for a lack of content, no letter, no anything else to leave. So indulge me as my testament is an infinite list of words packaged anxiously into homemade gifts to life: *Nan Dòmi* the Bible they will ever need; *Nothing Ever Dies*, so many buried alive already; *Lose your Mother* for home is nowhere; *The Lives of a Cell*, there are no reasons to go figure why in the country that nominates itself as the leader of the free world, freedom died itself out; and maybe the response to this immoderate question lays in *Hungry Translations*. *Do Tòti* will be their middle passage. Above all else not to forget, *Brother, I Am Dying*, their sole anthem.

Going to church

It begins like this:

I walk to the Café Latte on Grand Ave on most Sundays. I pull the heavy entrance door, march firmly towards a table slightly centering the eating room, and on the table, there sits a note that reads party of three. We are my book, my purse, and me. I transfer the sign to another table and quickly sit myself all the while holding my head straight up looking neither right nor left.

We are a party of stress, too. I will need to draw the outline of my teaching for the next day; a cup of regular coffee will push me through; a scone will give me some leverage.

I sit by the window. Any time soon an old couple will arrive on the left side of the room and swiftly sit themselves face to face. They will rub their salad with their forks, caress each other's hands with their touch, and eat each other's face. I am eyeing them. I will put on my OkC account 'must enjoy breakfast date'. The old couple seem to drink each other.

As for me, I'm mumbling. Which crime did the kids commit to be sent to church that same morning while I brought myself to Café Latte? They will have a party of penitence. At my Latte table, I will have some quiet time to read a few pages for my teaching. One rebirth themselves in rituals for the water that will soothe their thirst and for the collapse of the walls keeping them apart from themselves, from the beans, and from places they've walked. There is my black coffee I pay $2 something, the cup warming up my fingers, the flame and the smell of roasted beans, and a stress weighing high.

***

I dropped them at church early in the morning. At the entrance of the kids' arena, a church officer:

"Did you bring your bible?"

My *NO* is hasty, showy, and on purpose.

"Did you remember to bring offerings?"

I am very proud to say, *NO* the kids don't have offerings.

That's all I said, then the kids walk through the church's door, then the guilt I feel, then the frustration for not having said more to the church officer. Instead, I am leaving the church building for Café Latte. I am mad. And I am mad at myself. *Ce serait chouette d'avoir le sens de la reparti* and teach the kids how to talk back and not feel bullied or embarrassed for not bringing offerings or a bible to church—you know, the art of quipping fast; you besiege the enemy; make them take a step back; put on their lips a song never imagined; unsettle them. And you do that with offerings that contain more than a loud and proud *NO*.

My only revenge is leaving the building right after the kids enter their arena. I am proud to leave with my boots marching and sounding the floor for all to hear. I am not sneaking; I am just screaming, as other churchgoers enter the building for the morning service, you are not my people, I just need child care. I bring to the Café Latte table with me all I could have offered to the church soldier. I have no remorse, though, as I will sit down with the questions and the quips and the repartee, and service myself unbridled. One goes to church to connect with the god inside them. These questions, too, I guess will help me connect with the god inside me, on a table for a party of three, at a Café Latte table on Grand Ave in Saint Paul, all the church I needed then.

***

I knew a man who grew coffee for a living. He got paid a loaf of bread for his labor each day. Someday his own coffee ran bitter in his mouth and eating a piece of bread was like chewing himself up bone by bone. The loaf of bread could not save him. This is the story of a man who grew coffee for dying. He fell to his death one day among the coffee beans and, some would say, where he belongs. The coffee leaves received his body in their arms. This man, after all, spent his entire life growing beans up.

I dig into my coffee cup for a suitable outline for tomorrow's class. My eyes bear the color of the bottom of the cup. Maybe a writing exercise to begin the class? Well ... I did one last Wednesday, and the students are going to complain this course is just a chewing session. Don't be quick to assume a cup of coffee is a cup of beans. There are millions of stories of bodies who grow coffee for dying. Many chewed themselves up and have their bones chewed in china cups in big cities by big patrons; some fell on the sides of roads and on coffee leaves or got crushed up by pickup trucks vocationing themselves bringing beans to civilization.

No wonder a good dark roast cup of coffee is dark, dark, dark; dark with hands, arms, and body parts failing on coffee leaves; dark with stories flailing in the dark; a cup of dark coffee is more than what a small china mug befalls. I guess, a writing exercise, too. Like myself ruminating at a Café Latte table. The entire week it's been rushing to school, to the bus stop, to the food shelf, to the dinner table, to bathing, to teaching, to eating, to thinking, and to sleeping quick and quickly waking up the next morning to keep with the running. A pointless difference between the machine and the human is that the human can supposedly return and live their moments again and again. I try. I chew. I church. I'm on my own.

I am sipping my coffee as my eyes follow through the large windows folks going to church. For a moment, you think of trading your life with theirs. I take back this impulse right away. Drinking coffee is not growing beans. I am digging deeper into the bottom of my cup; my eyes and my days of running are in display. There are truths one must face, like trading a loaf of bread for 50 pounds of coffee beans or forcing my kids to go to church for some "me" time. I have to stop the running; a coffee leaf is grateful as hell.

I leave the Café Latte table at 11:45 to pick up Annie and Max. The kids are done by now but it does not hurt to let the church officers protect and serve for a little longer. I find my son sitting himself in a corner of the kids' arena; he hides his head between his shoulders. He is so very small all of a sudden. Am I the worst mom of all? I bend over him, I will never force you to go to church if you don't want to, I promise, except when they have toy giveaways. He is thinking the same thing, I bet, and he sighs to my words, a deliverance.

Although I sometimes deserve to stop running or take a deep breath away from kids, from church, and from other conventional penitence, I cannot keep taking profits from men growing coffee beans for a dying. I should know better.

***

We are exiting the church building. A prayer lady comes to us; we exchange hugs and kisses, and voice our blessings. *I love you.* I say I love you too. *I prayed for you.* I prayed for you, I say right back. She keeps her arms around my shoulders; she insists how I am holding on with her eyes un-mixed, clear, and prayerful; with her arms tightening my shoulders in a warm gentle squeeze. The kind of squeezing that translates into: are you hungry? Do you need groceries? Do you need someone to drop you off at home? How can we save you today? What's your name again? We gaze at each other. I am loving it. She is ready to recite a prayer over our shoulders right where we stand as she has done before; or maybe write us a check to put us to sleep for a few nights. We are doing awesome. The kind of awesomeness that is too nameless and too showy to be true. I have tons of things you can pray for, but it's not fair to have you build your penitence on my struggles. I am hungry for the right to reciprocity, that I can save you too from time to time, can you say my name?

***

The kids brought with them in the car their Sunday church pamphlet. The pamphlet shows the names and the pictures of several children: black and yellow and brown faces perfectly aligned on one of the sides of the glossy paper. At the bottom of each picture there is the story of the child. One of them has not eaten for days; another needs money to go to school; another is a victim of sexual assault, the list goes on; the great wars of the world are just a picture away. American kids are learning to save the world. Christopher Columbus and his fellow travelers played their part not so long ago when they murdered the Caribe natives and took their lands after planting the Christian cross in the bay of Môle Saint Nicolas.

We drive through Marshall Ave on our way home. At the Snelling intersection, a white fellow shows her cardboard sign: disabled and homeless, anything helps. We offer some snack bars and proceed. A bit further, at the corner of Marshall Ave and Lexington Ave, another young fellow holds his sign: two kids and a wife, anything helps. As I see many more signs lined up all along the avenue, I could feel the wars over here just a few blocks away from the kids' advertisement turning suddenly into a nicer picture. The church will need many more glossy papers to add the names of neighbors in need, I think out loud, which make my daughter sigh, roll her eyes. I always have something to say. In short, she is now transitioning.

We finally arrive at a stop light. I lift my derriere from my seat, lean on the brakes, and turn towards the kids—*you chil-*

dren listen—*it's like our apartment that is full of shit that we leave unattended, and we go to our our neighbors' houses, tell them they should clean up their messes; and we keep ourselves busy, and we push them to clean up, and we clean up their shit to the point we can no longer see nor smell the shit we make from our own corner.* In short, I was at the mercy of my own demons. And I owe my falling to aspire to certain human condition to my bare deprivation, my refusal to desire an unwanted penitence, and to the palpability of my own shit; all of this is a kind of imprisonment. I am fucked up. And the only thing thrilling about being fucked up is knowing that my life is fucked up and avoiding the kids' lives being fucked up by how fucked up my life has become. This is liberating, folks.

A few days before that Sunday, I was driving I-94E with my son in the back seat of our Toyota. Unexpectedly, I found myself gloating and rejoicing joyfully about the sudden awareness that my life is fucked up. Behind the wheels I voiced very loud, I don't give a fuck, plus many others thoughts that came along. You're reading this and you understand that I don't give a fuck about how fucked up my life is. But a split second after I said it, I realize my son was just telling me he doesn't like my humming, that he would rather have the radio on. See how fucked up I am? For I very well give a fuck about my son talking to me and telling me he doesn't like my chewing.

The dilemma of living in the Youwèsey is that a moment comes, and you realize you dwell in a state of permanent seizure, inadequacy, and humanlessness. You notice when the fingers move by themselves, when the breath outruns itself, and when your own past has forgotten your history. You see your sense of the everyday, your metaphysics, your ethics, and your ambiguous self, reduced to bare impulses, to touchability, to shit; all this is an afterlife palpable and livable nonetheless under the protection of the divine providence. This too is a kind of living. I keep up through coffee shots, every day, and some Sundays at the Café Latte on Grand Ave in Saint Paul, on a table that reads party of three, and we are my book, my purse, and me.

November 8
So, I am going to have trump for president for my golden birthday?

The woman stands frozen as she listens to her daughter's accusation. The moment is shitty. You want to walk out, like the smell under your armpits, the sweat running down your blouse, or the underneath of your stomach gutters you want to flee. But dwelling in is already a comfy deportment.

Before that, there was the presidential electoral campaign; the daughter would ask between one breath and the next what if trump wins, what if trump wins. She was at it with great details, taking note of what goes on with ribs, nose, larynx, lungs, esophagus and stuffy nose; things too familiar to care for, breathing shitting. She would bite her nails, her big eyes would pop out of her face, she would take a deep breath, and lift her chin abruptly the way the drowning victim realizes they are brought to life and to breathing all at once; and the woman would know the question was coming: what if trump wins? Each breathing moment is a silence interrupted by the uneasy feeling that no amount of air would ever be enough to the survivor brought back to life. It's a strange thing the way a sloth moves, in waves.

There were the stupid things the guy said, and there were his bullies. The daughter held cautiously in between her chest the fear that some of her friends may be asked to land on a shore they do not know. The moment is a tsunami behind each breath, a clash, waves that fill the lungs and wash away; what if trump wins.

A sloth senses things; things too near, things too far to take notice, things yet to happen; the way rip currents roll in and out darkened leaves, seashells, a pair of sunglasses, and watered washed away bodies. From the mushroom's ears to the return of the wave, a sloth pulses with things.

A child who holds the edge of the world at the tips of her nose and whose pain is displayed in her naked eyes, breathes things like a sloth.

***

The woman is haunted. American people are not that dumb, she throws at her daughter each time she drops in with her allegation. The woman would continue doing whatever else she was doing, caged in the waves of many shifts to reckon, like getting herself a tattoo at the neighborhood grocery store whose produce ran out. She also ponders whether it makes a difference having one candidate or the other for commander. Youwès democracy is a gigantic bag of sugar with holes at the bottom. One gets the same rat no matter what. For proof, Brazilian President Dilma Rousseff is packing her belongings while Filipinos are courting China, and the world is rolling.

The guy stands his grounds as a bully, a rapist, a flake, a fake no matter the rationale. The woman is locked up in her agitation as she curls and tightens her grip onto each thought, each sigh, each rape: her cage bars. She has been living on alien soil in her two-bedroom apartment with her two kids with no rush to marry or take an on-site associate for protection. At night, she sleeps with both eyes closed and does not worry a rapist, or a trumpist, or a *zenglendo* may break their door to move on them like a bitch, or grab'em by the pussy. She once said to an èks that his abuse and harassment hold criminal currency; this is the kind of dwelling she has found in the land of tonton sam. The guy winning would be another treachery, another rape, another assault. But the shame is already pouring down your blouse. You fled the horrors of the motherland only to face those of the alien soil. The moment stinks, but American people are not that dumb. They only lost the war some centuries ago and are still on the battlefield.

The daughter then, would hold her anxiety under her armpits until the return of the next wave, of the next breath to come back anew. And the woman chews and chews and chews and ruminates.

***

A stirring pleasure of the heart is to return to some life moments the way you pull drawers out of an abandoned dusty shelf, one after the other. You take a pause in between each drawer, in between each pull, in between each breathing to not leave behind the echo of the past, how it felt not so long ago, or a future rapidly fleeing.

The woman is helping her son with English composition. What is the color of the leaves? The son quickly plunges his right hand onto the sheet of paper as the pencil shrieks and tears up the composition sheet with a fierce, loud "red". The woman is pulled right back into her old days where you answer a question with a full sentence. The color of the leaves is red. The same for courting a girl, you make elaborate delicacies, you ask permission to advance, and you even write letters to show you got a brain that works. You don't just grab'em, even if what you want at the end of the day is to move on her like a bitch and then go on.

> the boars the jaguars and all human things a sloth
> gauges and stares
> a gradual winding down the
> breath by which the sloth returns
> as you arrive
> grab
> the sloth sitting and staring and
> warning the snake of a nearby hunter
> a sloth chews is
> how breath carries itself through.

The daughter brings home from school all kind of stories about the guy and how she and her classmates make fun of him. The entire classroom will vote for the woman. In her fellowship, the youngsters have a say and their tomorrow has already happened. The daughter also said she cannot yet get why a ten-year-old is not allowed to vote. What if the guy wins?
do you know he doesn't know how to read?
no—the mom says—I did not know that;
he said he will build a big wall;
When he hears that, the little brother standing nearby tightens his body and stares and screams at his sister with his eyes filled with horror, stop stop stop. He doesn't participate in his sister's obsession. But at the sound of "trump" and "big wall" tension grows in his body; his cheek pops out of his face; his ears shake, and his nose strikes with horror; his eyes are wild; his breathing comes in gasps with his entire body that slugs; then he leaves the room right away with all that. You could say he has the trump syndrome. This is usually the moment when the sister will, too, panic, but the second after, everyone is quiet, and the daughter tries to remember American people are not that dumb.

Her troubles for a moment find home under her armpits, one more time.

***

He has tiny hands. Everything about him is tiny, his dingaling, his brain, his fingers. But this is not why they hate him, that with his tiny hands and his small dingaling, he threatens to grab them by the pussy or that he calls them liar low energy crooked dummy rocket man. This is not either because he is mentally challenging and challenged and challenges to defund the Republic of Kindness. Of course, human wants are far greater and more complex than can be settled in in the confine of legalism. But politics, common senses, niceties, plus a relative sense of security are enough to turn a low burlesque show into the truest performance of all.

Youwès democracy is the privileged spouse who enjoys through legalism the right to abuse its spouse.

In a conventionally good union, the wife hides bruises and blackened eyes and a tortured soul under the security of the husband's blanket. The battered woman goes to the police and is told this is your husband, deal with it, take things in, swallow your pride, or just go to sleep. In the marriage, a rape is not a rape, the husband has rights, privileges, and power. Youwès democracy cannot work without church churching the crooked female spouses that their bodies belong to their husbands, to their nation, to God; without the constitution summoning its citizens to call the police; without the schools teaching the children the features of the stranger. Youwès democracy is a show circus which includes the parade of American dreams for some and the parades of its greatness for the corporatist *sans-terre*. Genocide and rapes and mass killings and hunger is another parade of another sort in the same show circus; but under the banner of law and democracy they are not rapes, genocide, black killings, and hunger; they're just bad things that happen to bad people.

You let yourself linger. And you ruminate and chew with the woman. You are angry and you agree it's all parades, niceties, and show circuses all along. The female candidate as president is the promise of a better act, the show shall go on. The bully in office is a bad marriage with a rebellious shameless wife who fails to act but show The People the true visage of their union.

After all, no system of governance is perfect. But that Youwès Democracy is about maintaining unshaken inequality is the ultimate slap Americans cannot endure, certainly not now. But a wave doesn't come all at once, and one never knows when the slap is on its way. The woman cannot take the slap, either. She ran away from home so her daughter can be a free spirit who swings her hips in the direction she chooses. She is convinced that The People are not that dumb. They owe it at least to her to prove to the world they condemn the name callings, the grabbing 'em by the pussy, and all other banter talks.

It's a good thing a sloth does not go to school after all to learn about *demokrasi*. They would never notice the arrival of the predator. How do you think they survive?

***

Democracy: noun; definition:
The slave shouts *enough is enough*
kicks the master's ass for good
sending him all the way back to his homeland;

the master whispers,
depi nan Ginen nèg rayi nèg
Suze Matthiew swears:
Depi nan Ginen nèg renmen nèg;

but then the slave turned royalty declares over his kingdom:
all crops for the market,
befriends the master
who has only swapped a yellow suit
for a blue one when landed home
all the while staying on top of the market trunk;
And it seems to be the old slave
who now gives away the land meter by meter
one slave after another
under the protection of Youwès law.

***

The woman goes to school I heard. She gets out of bed at 5:00 each morning then walks and dives right to her work. In the hours that follow, her shoulders are bent and her fingers hit the keyboard tic tac tic tac. She sighs. And she fuels her stomach with several shots of coffee, nonstop. Her neck is stiff; her arms, her hands, and her fingers jostle as if they have feet of their own. It is that her body is already taken away from her, and, for no apparent reason, her heartbeats echo the whittling of her bones she carries straight up under the pretense of coping courageously. She's afraid of falling off herself. Then the hope that drags her down: in a couple of weeks her life will become normal again; she will recover from the heartbeats that go sometimes too fast, sometimes too slow, so often so unevenly; from the fingers that move by themselves when she's not on the keyboard; and from the neck that sores in permanence; the elections is rarely mentioned here. She's on the finish line for her own exams, and she's happy despite her body being robbed from her, bit by bit. And you hear the woman say *my body is my testament*. What a great journey of punishment to get in exchange of martyrdom.

A few months before, the woman had replaced her large size bed with a twin size to have an office in her bedroom. So before walking out of her chamber each morning, she cages herself into her work the way you see a bird entering a cage, one wing swinging the other forth, with a certain poise, and the door closes behind them. The woman will pass her exams, under siege, with several cups of coffee nights and days. It hurts inside the chests. In the evening, she lights up the air with some good laugh. She also voices to herself that she has willingly entered the cage, that she holds between her fingers the keys to her cell, a trick as old as the history of oppression or liberation or both. The big show she makes out of everything. Then she goes to bed, lies on her back with her palms at her mouth and cracking up: the 2016 Youwès election is between Alec Baldwin and Kate McKinnon. In the morning that follows, she goes running again.

When a woman carries on one breath after the other, she goes after the entire world. American people are not that dumb. It was during the fall she made sure all her papers are solid enough to win her her own candidacy. She wasn't thinking about anyone else's future and her heartbeat was out of its rhythm.

The day of the presidential elections she will email her doctoral committee members an electronic copy of each of her exam documents. She enters into her sleep each night like the defeated valiant soldier who will not let go of the battlefield. She too has a war, an election to win. She is that miserable. After all, all she wants is for the heart to calm down.

Now you're thinking how tricky it is to think about the kind of wars that really matter in those election days. Whether it's being in the world like a sloth perching over their branches and on the lookout or hitting the keyboard in an office bedroom by way of coffee shots. This is a tricky question, the same breath, and another kind of wave.

***

How long has it been already?

My friend Z lives not too far from our apartment, invites us over for dinner, the Mississippi River is a few blocks away, the elections are everywhere in every minute. We could feel it filling up the air like an oversaturated balloon made up of massive steel. It is as thick as you imagine it to be, so you pull yourself up and make all sorts of laudable resolutions: who cares anyway? The kids and I show up around 7:30 to dine not to TV. My inner torment is in line with the disturbances coming from the TV screen in the living room. We are thinking about the elections but feel triumphant not talking about the elections. We're here for food, friendship, and resignation.

Many in our community, Z included, have done all they could to leak, poke, blow the balloon in all possible directions with no success. We get what we get. The kids dig into green beans cooked in chicken curry sauce and white rice. They will complain tomorrow how my food sucks. Eating a delicious meal is a pleasure I can understand. Notes to myself now: I will learn new recipes after I pass my own exams. I sigh loudly in front of green beans cooked in chicken curry sauce and white rice. My friend Z is a good cook. It's a unique night tonight, our spirit won't be broken.

the grievances
the owl has not yet called
my tears
the night we miss
the promises

Everything always goes great in my life is the kind of wall I do not put up with. I count my blessings. I complain. I walk naked. I play tricks with myself to get stuff out. I do not hide my misfortunes. Be my voyeur for a moment is all the change I ask. But I don't want you to do a thing about things you cannot do anything about. Don't go thinking you can save me. Save yourself is all for you to do. I pour myself out in front of Z, complain about weariness and fatigue and she does something about it. We do yoga on the floor. Z is the kindest friend I have. Yoga is a wall builder and its walls are echo full and leaking. I cannot not notice the big TV screen. We're watching the elections among other things among other talks and among our doing yoga. I am kind of okay with that, we all give change for something else. I am not okay with the race being so far away but so tight and so near. There's not a thing yoga can do about the fullness of a race locking you up in between its walls as thick as time made of all times.

The kids and I left Z's house around 9 pm with a self-taught yoga DVD, leftovers, the walls have been up for as far as we could remember.

you do not vote
to bed she goes hopeful the land
her armpits

November 9, 2016. The earth continues its rolling. Now how does one write an email, send documents, make the morning bed or brew the coffee in the midst of an earthquake? I slip under my covers. Against overwhelming odds, I have not yet heard anything. The hands that scratch and moan will take the plea for the flea, by mistake only.

**

The woman's next race is to explain to her kids that one does not heat together the milk with the coffee to get café-au-lait but they could. After all she's never had an answer to the daughter's question. What if trump wins? When heated together, the curdled milk resting at the top of the café-au-lait is repugnant and hideous; the kind of waste, your shit, you do not want to own. You do not tell your host at the dinner party that their food has turned your stomach. Plus, there are reasons why your colored friends are not around the table with you sharing the moment. You get along so very well. You get along so very well apart. Then you heat the milk and the coffee separately, then you bring them together accordingly: they've always belonged to each other without being a reflection of each other. What a delicious coffee! Isn't the weather beautiful today! The kids will learn about the elections result at school or in the bus or at recess or whenever. A curdled milk is neither milk nor cheese. The woman walks out of her bedroom like a convict worker partially deprived of her freedom. She is on pause.

The kids, fully dressed up and fully anxious, snack around the small kitchen table. The world is not at rest but this is not a reason to mix café-au-lait with café latte in the microwave.

He won ... you know ... unfortunately;

That's it? This is all she can say to apologize for false hope? Her breath carried across their phantom bodies unfulfilled desires, saddened love, and false confessions.

How come? People don't love him?

Next time we'll do better, we'll get involved, we'll help get the word out just like our friends did.

And the daughter cries, and the woman cries, and the little boy cries. They cry, they weep, they sob life is not fair. Tears envelop their lifeless shoulders. The sky was gray. It was a frightening realization, a treachery in display: the key holder enters the stage noisily, shows up their face, and turns abruptly the key after the prisoners have entered the confines. The key holder has no body attached to it. It was there all along.

I don't need trump for president.

The daughter is tearing up but it's not like her water owns her.

Maybe he'll be in office for one year only, maybe he'll be impeached ...

The woman stops suddenly in her derive, she should know better and she says right away to her daughter that four years pass quickly. The woman is learning not to sink into her own agitation.

But four years is too long.

The woman does not know anymore what to say. The daughter screams louder and louder.

I am going to have trump for president for my golden birthday?

The woman could no longer pull herself back up; there was nothing she could say to make things right for her, for her daughter, for her son.

Why can't kids vote for president . . . all my classmates would have voted for her.

The daughter chews again and again and again that morning of November 9, 2016.

A few minutes later the woman puts the kids in their school bus. She then goes back to her kitchen table, writes a note to her friend: I shouldn't be writing this morning. I want to let go all of me, my chest, my breather, my body, let go of all of it, my water, my blood, and sink faster, lower, deeper, the way leaves, seashells, and walking sticks offers themselves to the waves of violent seas. I have gone mad. You see, I am neither a victim nor victor. For the first time I see myself as an American and we don't deserve this shit, this shit, and this shit. I just don't know what else to say. As Americans, we are not that dumb, we are just busy fighting our battles, talking to the wrong crowds, obsessing over the weather, the summer, the coffee, not returning on our wastes before moving on.

For the first time the woman is breathing on the wave of the sloth.

Youwenvibriyokoleraedefinisyion

DouzJanvye

Faultlines

Tremblemandtè

316.000

goudougoudou

Pòtoprens

sixhomes

goudougoudou

Youwenvibriyokoleraedefinisyion

Douzjanvye

Faultlines

Earthquake

minisatakolera

-2-
Three Apertures

1.

Why are we having all these people from shithole countries come here?
The troubled white man is confused between continents, ge-ography lines, and his toes going out of sight before him. Un-derneath his belly, history books are packing their belonging, and the man to think he's wrapping within an entire civilization. His-story is hysterical. You pass through sea cycles, waiting rooms, sugar cane plantations, from and to Ayiti by way of the transat-lantic, plus the non-retour to Africa, nothing pours out. In the man's conveniences, history is swollen, bloated like a balloon to the point you want to sticks your fingers into its flanks. So, when Youwès tags Haiti or San Salvador or Africa as shithole countries it's not that their illusion made me historical, simply that mem-ory frowns upon time against its will and latch things off.

A major complication of crossing the transatlantic is to stand before waste. I cannot stop thinking about bodies wasted in the middle of the ocean, a fading *New York Times* article on the City of Philadelphia unloading its waste in the port of Gonaives, or my mother and father journeying into their own waste. CIA, the accounts say, penetrated Haiti with high quality genetic stocks in pig, chickens, and humans of a certain creed, making rooms for Bill to dump in the waste of the Arkansas farmers. The "uses of Haiti", Paul Farmer who isn't from Arkansas calls the entire dumping operation. And just yesterday, a Youwèn cargo pours its ways into the waters of the l'Artibonite and 10,000 dead bodies poured back, forfeiting themselves into the ashes of history. I come from a shithole. That the shit is my own or someone else's is not where the real story begins. It's true that at some point all of us have to go back to how the tail of our shit diverges from the trail of another's, and the geography holes they make. But this is not the matter at hand. Here and now I am ambushed in a shit sea and obliged to step forward. In the radius of my sea cycle always changing, always shifting, and always shitting, I do not dream of removing myself from the shit sea. All to do is get a grip on the shit and bring it into your living room.

Still, so many wars and scars and battlefields to uncover as I quickly avert my eyes from waste circuses. I wipe off of my shoes all the shit, as if this is all yours to deal with. Unwanted cargo. I am sorry to hurt your feelings, I would like to say. And I go from me to you in a derangement of a shit cycle. You won't show yourself naked; I come to you unguarded. You're uneasy; I am shameless. You have much to lose; I've already lost everything there was to lose. The matter is, you cannot put a face to a piece of feces. Your shit has no longitude no latitude. The doctor will ask you to bring a tiny piece of your stool to her lab, not your entire landscape, so that each centimeter of my fecal matter is the face of my stool, and the face of you too. My geography tells a whole lot about you. In a sea of shit and memory pits at times going in circle and more often breaking away, no one can run from their undesirable cargo, whether you are an orangish dude worth millions of green or a banana farmer president. In the shit sea I stand to take my turn, wander, and face up my waste with a queer kind of feeling of catching up with old scents. See what I mean?

2.

George Floyd is pinned to the ground by the neck for eight minutes and forty-six seconds. The ten-minute video is like a century blanket thrown over the landscape of the 17th, 18th, and 19th centuries America. May 25, 2020, ropes them all together, but with no assumption that the breath on the ground has anything to do with the breadth of promises of new eras; George Floyd was death before his death.

A black man murdered by justice, by his fellow humans, remains forever larger than how the sky covering his city, his family, his bread catalogues him. It isn't just a concept that his aroma, breathing, and saliva coat together the asphalts of 38th Street and Chicago Avenue from 56th Flatbush to 20 Rue Guerrier passing by 13 Rue du Commerce. The black man pours himself out as water might pour from a jarring sea. All of us, like a clear picture on a glossy page of the latest *Vogue* stand as we have always stood, so clean and so neat and so supposedly free. And we're still standing. And this is the part I often wonder about. Of course, Floyd is in some way each one of us and larger than the pieces of his life pulled together by a soul-shaking inhuman operation that went disturbing the quietness of a civilization peoples very much in love of themselves. Floyd was never supposed to go wander free. He was never supposed to put himself on parade for all to see freedom as black, as naked, as raw and unguarded. I suppose he may just have been one of the negroes in Gwendolyn Brooks' poem "Riot":

Because the Negroes were coming down the street.

Because the Poor were sweaty and unpretty
(not like Two Dainty Negroes in Winnetka)
and they were coming toward him in rough ranks.
In seas. In windsweep. They were black and loud.
And not detainable. And not discreet.

A consortium of neatly covered fellows is put out naked in the street for all to see, they're hurt. When an exposed fellow is hurt, he clothes himself right back, then goes right away in the street to put out shame, guilt, anger, and ecstasy. He pours himself as history. Underneath of all that I see the thrill of the truth: the self is its own enemy, any self is an enemy of another self, an enemy of humanity. A black man carefully shutdown for all to see and who, as far as we know, could have gone in history books as an absence, holds now the particles of a century already gone.

The horror that follows can offer a ride one should ride as much and as long as they can, but without confounding the ride for the thing itself. That the revolution is the revolution is a matter of approach. But any maroon or resurgent or looter knows that revolution as crack, as blow, or as the thing in itself is an allegiance to family tree, to persona, and consortium in their very shinny attires. And any being who lives in the contradictions and interpellations of things knows that they can't vow allegiance to crack, to stillness, and cleanness. One then rather clothe themselves with dirt, with nakedness, and smelly breath.

Like you walk your way to the university office, load your back pack with a sack of chocolates for home, which is more than your usual dosage; take from the administration office a bottle of hand sanitizer, a few tea bags, a roll of toilet paper, plus a ram of office paper, all for home. The way some, all of a sudden see themselves walking and entering a Target neighborhood and pack as much as clothes, body lotions, and raw meats their bony bodies can carry to see themselves called looters and punishable to death by the university police. Yours is a looting of the same sort, but neatly covered up and glorified, given that stealing is by agreement the only possible relationship with the university consortium. Anyway, who doesn't loot?

Out of the blue, city counties fund the poor for rent, for food, for doctor visits and for everything else imagined. Rent Relief assistance is available for the three next months. The graduate student office unexpectedly operates stimulus pocket funds for summer grads. The stranger at the grocery store is astutely pulling up a friendship package from the alien's almond glazed oranges candy. Membership packages and music lessons are giveaways. Free smells here. Street Arts for George. I can't breathe. The poor, the alien, the brown body are suddenly eligible for citizenship status, ranks, apertures, and privileges, and supposedly brought back to life. The Department is now accepting applications for the 1930 Marilla-Pérez Graduate Fellowship, named after graduate student and activist Marilla-Pérez who died by suicide. See? Any consortium always takes more and in disproportionate proportion to its giving. For before all that parade, the killing didn't happen all at once, but ran itself on a process of small, daily cracks, terrors, damnation, and fears visible in every students' halls, in leftover kitchens, on the subway station, in every administration, in the hiring of a new chair, in the new dean's speeches more sensibly tailored, in every new promise of revolution, in youngsters slowly giving themselves to madness for having accumulated too many shifts in their brains, in students slowly roping themselves through the nodes of their backs, necks, and bones. That sort of life and many more that make a fellow death before his death. The crack of being, of what the university or any humane project is about (two of the police officers charged in Floyd's murder were students at the University of Minnesota; Derek Chauvin whose knee held Floyd's neck on the ground attended Metro State University in Saint-Paul-Minnesota) seems to hold itself in the struggles between terror and freedom, between possibilities and impossibilities, between self and others, so that the opposite of freedom is not bondage.

Looters and maroons freed themselves in the colony of St. Domingue and carried on their back like their former holders, the thirst to hold others captive. Freedom from bondage doesn't put them in any confederation. Having inhabited the lower side of power, they learn against their dangerous selves that the powerless are powerful. Those on the upper side of power lives in the illusion of power with the disadvantage of fighting a battle they think they can control. The maroon fights a battle she knows is bigger than herself. Both the powerful and the maroon have in common to stand against the course of history, against the course of time, and with the inhuman in the human. So, a maroon remains a maroon, at all time for their own sake, and not so much for love of fairness and justice. This is why the maroon is not afraid of the judgement of power which never fails to come equally from all creeds, from all traces, and from all races and geographies. To save herself the maroon gives herself to madness, to folly, and to malignant odors. She outruns death in its own course. On a ride too wild and too wide to control, she saves herself from death by subjecting death to itself. Being a maroon, if there's such a thing, is not a forever condition, as any system sooner or later cracks, recomposes, and balances itself in and out of cracks. In an equal proportion, revolution, independence, freedom and war is always something undone, unfinished, and unseen.

You negate me my humanity, the black tenant writes to the proud POC building leader who fines her ass for good under some legalistic principle without giving her the chance of a hearing. She signed off almost: "I can't breathe." In Brooks's "Riot" the smell of staunch smoky negro bodies was repugnant enough to lit the sky in fire:

John Cabot went down in the smoke and fire
and broken glass and blood, and he cried "Lord!
Forgive these nigguhs that know not what they do."

3.
The breed

All of them sat; their feet touching the curling flame of the burning woods; the weight of their body dropping to rest farting the
flicking air every minute or so in their repose after a long day
road-tripping; a rare gateway for brothas and sistas who make
their practice to silently peacefully decay; elucidating one's her-
itage is the most distasteful gesture there is; Tanesha dropped
herself against a background as dark as nights as silences as
times so wide and so very dark you could walk a century and
never be able to separate nights from days; I didn't know I was
to do breathing Tanesha puffed; that I was made up to breathe;
not that tonight the pigs should be fed lards cooked in rice and
grass and beans; I shouldn't get used to breathing; and Tanesha keeps pushing the dark into the background or depending
on one's mirroring reflection the background into the dark; and
Jabbar said I am more peaceful than all of you put together; it's
the librium no it's the hydroxyzine; it's every time Megan is at
the beach or by the lake or with family reunionning; I look at the
photos and the beautiful sunset and the beautiful faces pop up
on my screen to show what a beautiful life looks like to see myself tranquil and peaceful; how did I come to bargain Covid-19
for I can't breathe and out-screen myself by the lake and feel
the breeze and breathe better, see?; and Moriah said to Jabbar
too bad you can't get *poulets-aux-hormones* for sleepeaceness;
Neri jumped that she wishes we stopped inducing into coma
with dose of Vyvanse little brains who can't learn schoolshit;
she needs to remember she says to tell her sister not to tie her
schizophrenic other little sister to a chair or turn her stomach
into world's most largest drugstore but to let her walk her walks
however miles away she wants as she is probably walking up to
these regions of life one would rather forget or leave behind; it
was as if Neri was saying to Jabbar he is just buying himself time
and working hard to purchase one day the Alabama plantation
he was born on and send pics to his Dakota friend; and Ebony
and Chaquille and Darius take turn at throwing allegiance to
peace which then turn into another contest of another sort like
between black here and black from another planet; Carmelle
says Remember I-can't-remember-her-name who wore her hair

short and braided year round, ate fufu all day, and clothed her-self in flashy yellow red blue stripes and so black and scream-ing you ain't black enough; George who was silently mixing his breathing into the fire cracking said it's the lineage; there isn't any other breed more peaceful more accommodating and more cooperative than those beloved of whom they killed the broth-er and whose children, mothers, fathers, and sisters sit still, in peace, in love, in hope, and so unapologetically pushing away anger and bitterness or let's say apologetically bittering and rag-ing peacefully within; you see a police precinct, a restaurant, and a neighborhood grocery store catching fire in the midst of their raging tranquilizing medicated anger and they still find a way to peace; it's the other camp not us; in the campfire burning at their feet, large pieces of woods abruptly dropped themselves each minute, burnt themselves out slowly, then remained in the shadows before kindly disappearing; not at all in the rhythms of jubilant flames dancing across feet and farts and flames; more like an intimate warring anarchy where coups of all kinds are permitted and where the fickle of the first burning wood is peacefully carried across by other leftover rested bodies breez-ing and breathing.

-3-
You May Have the Suitcase Now

February 1986

I remember this dress my mother had. A salmon-pink dress, loose, and gradually wider towards the bottom. I watched her in that dress facing the crowd invading our house the morning of February 7, 1986. *Nou mèt pran sa nou vle*, she hurls as she opens the entrance door. The crowd poured in. Was she shocked to see Man Ato among them? Maybe they won't harm anyone, she must have said to herself. The salmon-pink dress was floating around her legs following each of her movements. The women in the crowd also wore large dresses that they turned into containers as they filled them up with plates, tablecloths, silverware, and angry hopes. There was, through the door slit, the sway of the dress gripping me softly, a womb of memory I am trapped inside.

The entire week we heard waves of people marching down Rue Guerrier from house to house, putting them in ruin, and chanting *bay tè a blanch*. A month earlier, my brother, Baudelaire, and I strolled and hopped and tootled down the same street en route to Pastè Lubin's school. I was 7, he was 8, and the two of us already grown out of the edge of childhood. From far away Mom waved us goodbye while cracking jokes with Man Ato. Between the pages of our books, my brother and I would place cassava and biscuits to secretly toss into our mouths while the teacher goes on and on about multiplication and division tables. At recess we occasionally stop by the *machann Ak-100* for our lunch. Then February came out, made a show of himself. Rue Guerrier was covered with dust and the *machann Ak-100* was nowhere to be found. On Radio Soleil, song *Lè m pa wè solèy la* was released. No one knew who the singer was, but many were arrested when caught singing "I am up to no good when the sun does not show up" in the streets. People were stirring up the last drop of their anger, talking relentlessly and freely for all to hear about overthrowing Jean-Claude Duvalier. Those working in his government would be unleashed, too.

We locked ourselves into an isolated bedroom that morning of February 7. We jolted at the drives of stones smashing, at our heartbeats pounding, at our fists clutching into one another. My mom, wrapped in her troubled salmon-pink dress, followed the ground quaking under our feet, while our life, dreams, and silverware were being packaged into other large dresses, none of them salmon-pink. Later that day Mother rolled up her leftover self in leftover bed sheets, tablecloths, linen, toothbrushes, new and worn-out shoes, and crispy fried goat. On the radio, the United States government has taken things in hand: Baby Doc is overthrown. We left Saint Michel to Port-au-Prince a few months later. In my mom's suitcase, the uneasy salmon-pink dress and the remains of a slice of time wait for a new home.

Today, I carry a suitcase of my own. I have become very familiar with its weight, its odors, and damaged corners. Whenever I shut myself up in my kitchen in our Saint Paul two-bedroom with a notebook, I rummage through, dig, and draw out from inside its contours the secret wounds, the fears, and the memories of a world long ago forgotten. A world which begins in that Rue Guerrier house in Saint Michel de l'Attalaye. Each afternoon, my butt cheeks rest on the ground and my head camps in between my mom's knees. Mother is braiding my hair, her own bottom sitting on the green wooden canape. All of me stays locked between her two feet. If I move right or left, I receive a slap on the shoulders or something sharper, the comb, will bite my back in tune with my mom's voice, *kenbe tèt ou dwat!* She is planting cornrows on the scalp of my head: the first strand is for "*Nan ou menm ki genyen lavi*" from the Chants d'Espérance, the second for "*A l'arrivée de l'expédition Française envoyée par Bonaparte*" from our favorite history book, and the third for "*Pour le pays pour les ancêtres mourir est beau*" which begins the national anthem. Our childhood is here, anchored in the praise of suffering (why we need God), veneration of school (because we are France's children), and devotion to the homeland (for which death is an honor). We left Saint Michel to Port-au-Prince from this place of faith, power, and impotence. God will provide.

We crossed over the river Savann Dezole. The bus quaked, rolled, and trundled through Pont Lestè above ragged pavements that put our derrieres in tandem with not knowing what's ahead. I sit by the window; my chin is on my pillow. If we fall off the bridge it will be like slightly transitioning to a lower level of the road. But Mother's suitcase is elegiac, and going to live in Port-au-Prince is more like emerging suddenly on a highway. I am threaded through the river's passage of low bushes and stones drying up.

Some decades later, I watch from a computer screen Baby Doc's presidential procession making its way through the Haile Selassie airport among a crowd of curious feet walking to know first-hand if this is it. A few cars one after the other, the in-laws and, at the end of the cortege, a president for life, stripped of his power, with his wife and their suitcases. The exit is troublesome and awkward; the power that vanishes, the estates, then the royal gowns, and the mannerisms, too. A fallen god quitting the stage under the camera flashes, like an abjured servant dragging a painful burden. The dethroned president for life boarded a United States Air Force jet and fled to France as my father is thrown to Port-au-Prince the same day. Today Savann Dezole runs dry.

And Somewhere Over the Rainbow

a suitcase gives vent to the echoes of doors cutting through the slits time makes. Whether this suitcase is the valise of those leaving before the curtains touch the floor, the dark green helmet of a handsome *tonton makout*, or the screen from which I watch the overthrow of Baby Doc to remember my mom's little salmon-on-pink dress and my father's exile.

On the computer screen, I glare at several pages, sigh as my daughter walks by, I will call my dad. Twenty-five years ago, he arrived in Port-au-Prince through Marmont and NanPaul carrying his own suitcase. I have a photograph of him holding onto a microphone. He is a handsome middle-aged man with stark dark skin; he hides his sparkly eyes behind a pair of sunglasses. He is not smiling but has his lips pursed. The upper lip presses the lower one tightly. You mimic with your own lips and wonder if he's about to speak or if he is just swallowing himself up. The picture may have been taken at a public gathering. He'd preside over tons of them in the park or at a corner of the public market near the Simoncomte Boutik. My father's biggest weakness is his awareness of his power in the way he carries himself. His march is elegant and equal to those of the horses that accompanied him from one place to another. The sound of the horses' hooves trotting each time he returns from his crusades echoed my father moving through the world as a pastor, community organizer, advocate, government worker, and schoolteacher. He wished he could change the world.

Sitting in front of a computer is like walking the edges of many worlds. Duvalier had landed in Port-au-Prince after Twenty-five years in exile. In a wave of massive protests, Egypt's Hosni Mubarak steps down following thirty years in office. Pope John Paul II is promoted to Sainthood; did he visit Mubarak as he did for Duvalier before the 1986 overthrow? The airport from which a massive crowd salutes the return of Duvalier has become the Toussaint Louverture International Airport. So much goes on from Ethiopia's Haile Selassie to Haiti's International Louverture that a name swapping won't show: the math of connection. At this place of merging grounds is a suitcase in display whose pockets will not tell how unlife the load has been. Pairs of pants, a silk black dress, sugarcanes, cacao, fault-lines, cellphones, notebooks, melatonin, and scars.

    As far as I can remember it was my mother unleashing herself like a refrain, "*we were thrown into Port-au-Prince.*" I am the history of stones sprawling out of waterless rivers. I cannot bring myself to arrange these instances properly. I am not proper. This I understand as I am scheduled to do a presentation on Haiti to a group of students in Saint Paul and for which I am pulled into my earliest memory: I am a five-year-old again and going to school with Baudelaire in Saint Michel and walking in the morning dew. Early afternoon we chase birds with *fistibal* and dig into the ground of our backyard for sweet potatoes. We fill several bins of mangoes that fell from the trees the night before. Passersby join and sit with us around large bins of *mango tikawòt, mango blan, mango misca, mango fransik.* We ate most of them; the bulging ones will land in the kitchen to be turned into mango jam. The sugar canes are the best of all, rushing down our throats like waterfalls. The smell of each morning dew carries the trail of fresh fruits and vegetables, and there for all to see, ground sprouting mangoes, coffee, avocados, and *diri latibonit*.

There are no artifacts to show that my life is not in history books. Over the years my travel-size luggage has been reduced to a small valise of old journals and letters turning yellow, the home of old IDs, expired passports, and birth certificates. It is now the size of a small folder, but in truth, my suitcase is lidless. I will mimic in front of my students the kind of report Christopher Columbus gave to queen Isabella on Santo Domingo. I will crumple a piece of paper to stage the features of this corner of the world with rich rainforests, mountains, and abundant water and food resources. Columbus may have had laid his feet in Saint Michel de L'Attalaye. You caught me, Yip Harburg, *somewhere over the rainbow, blue birds fly*.

Shits, Holes, and Rue Tiremasse

Following the 1986 overthrow, we arrive in Port-au-Prince where narrowed corridors outnumber cracked pavements and BP fumes cover for Saint Michel's morning dew. Every year, and sometimes after a few months of settling in a new quarter, we would move to another quarter, from one neighborhood to another, drawing ourselves a bit closer to another edge of the moon. With each move, we wrap ourselves and our clothes and linens in large plastic bags that we drag behind us. We sometimes use our pillow cases to pack things in. We throw them and we throw ourselves into the back of large pickup trucks that will carry us to our next place. There were no bus tickets of any sorts to put on record those movements to Delmas 6, Delmas 33, Delmas 31, or Rue Tiremasse. I remember school bands marching, roses walling the walls of Saint-Louis de Conzague, a St Jude's medical station, numerous bric-à-bracs and *bank bòlèt*, and almond trees in each corner. We have carried the steam of these places, their cracked pavements, sandbags and almond skulls under the soles of our feet, in our lidless suitcases.

Rue Tiremasse, among many other places we roamed, is a *dépotoir*, a dumping ground, a place of merging geographies. In its intersections lie several monuments of waste we jokingly call Christmas trees for their tall height, their triangular shape, and multicolor lines coming from unwanted garlands of plantain peels and ripe bananas. The monuments are also decorated with tomatoes in tatters; bottles and cans of vegetable oils and foods of all kinds stamped "Made in USA"; food packaging, Miami-Rice bags, The New York Times crosswords pages and newspapers and magazines are front-row seated, star-like; plus many other things lying on top of each other; but that's not all. Every morning, in one of Rue Tiremasse's corners, a *machann pèpè* hangs on the street walls pieces of clothes one by one; skirts, long and short sleeve shirts, corsages, underwear of all shapes and sizes; nights out outfits, workhouse dresses, business clothes, moccasins, sandals, and leather shoes; two-piece suits, some almost new, some with spots and stains; others that reek of smoke; pairs of sunglasses, flashlights, and silverware; there are also not so random boxes of Dark & Lovely perm. On the opposite side of the same wall the *machann pèpè* places t-shirts of many colors that stand one chest after the other; the reds are together and then the yellows and then the blacks and then the grays. They are wrinkly from being stuffed together in *pèpè balls*, their own suitcase. On top of that, another pile of clothes sits on the ground that the *machan pèpè* gives away throughout the morning for a dollar or two; the armpits and the neck areas nest the sweats and the stains of their previous owners. They read "In God We Trust" or "Welcome To NY."

In one of these corners of Rue Tiremasse, a mountain of Miami rice cooked in *pwa kongo* and lards sits in a large pan. The *machann pèpè* is a *machann aleken*. In the middle of the day, workers in suits and ties will sit among the piles and the walls of clothing for their lunch. A radio laying at the feet of the *machann pèpè* and the customers will bring the news, the time of day, the music of the hour, and everything else to know. Everything to live for is right here in this corner of Rue Tiremasse filled with mufflers roaring, with *aleken* steaming, with clothes sweating cigarette smoke, salivas, stains, and traces from every corner of the world and unleashed by the *machann pèpè* each morning after journeying from closed dark closeted storages in the Youwès.

Most afternoons, we have rendezvous with the *machann kann* arriving from Léogane to sell sugarcane sticks. He will take possession of one of Rue Tiremasse's intersections for a good half hour. He stands on his two feet splayed in parallel to those of his cart full of sugar canes. His right knee is slightly bent. In this half hour, he is the knight on his horse who embarks on a high-stakes duel. He removes swiftly each sugarcane stick out of its sheath, peels rapidly one stick after the other with a long sharp knife, turns hastily each stick upside down, flips it at the bottom, then right again from the top. His fencing armor is nothing more than a t-shirt and short pants and the sweat running through his spine. In just a few seconds he trades his long ready-to-chew sticks of sugarcane against a few cents of ours. We have an afternoon sitting on our balcony and filling our gut with sugar canes and slurping slurp, slurp, slurp.

Sometimes it was the *machann fritay* selling fried plantains, hot dogs, and grilled pork at the same intersection. From our balcony, the radio gives off Jocelyne Beroard's *Zouk La Se Sèl Medikaman Nou Ni* and *Kole Sere* or news of the Bush administration welcoming Haiti's newly freely elected president. We pick our lemons and avocados in the street market, and boiled eggs *aux hormones* cloned in USA take over Saint Michel's Ak-100 and *kassava-a-mamba*. To live in Rue Tiremasse was to walk daily through the common denominator among our roaming with Saint-Michel ghosting and patching things up.

My dad works relentlessly at growing papayas and cherries in our front yard; underneath his palms the ground fights and rebels. Father keeps planting and adding to the traces, the sweats, and the smells of Port-au-Prince to behold his dream from the steams of the Miami-Rice rising from the *machann pèpè*'s. This is Rue Tiremasse, which looks like a corner of Saint Paul where I carry myself sometimes to catch the scent of cassava, of *mango fransik,* and the bitter taste of my father's discontent.

Pèjo

I don't want beans for dinner, my daughter complains from her bedroom. My son echoes. *But beans carry lots of proteins*, my dad would say. *Tomorrow morning*—and I scream from my kitchen table—*we will bike by the river*, which I know you don't like, for you'd rather spend your day with your electronics; we'll go anyway. I don't want you to take the Mississippi river, its falls, and cottons for granted. Savann Dezole dried up a long time ago. "*My tablet is dead, I cannot find my charger*," my daughter screams; between silences, keyboard chews, and times stretched: "*I have lost my purpose. Can I use your computer?*" But I am busy with the computer. Later in the afternoon, I will take a walk to clear my head about why I can't go a day without my computer. There's no mistake in living behind for a while the future I had some twenty years ago.

Early mornings on Saturdays, my dad drives my mom and all of us *anbalavil* to buy fresh fruits, vegetables, goat meats, and the beefs balls they will ask us not to eat. Beefs balls are not for girls and would make us want to have sex, we children believed our parents were thinking. We make the Saturday trip in a sort of gray-green Jeep my father will trade later for a Mitsubishi pick-up truck. We arrive *anbalavil* and park the car somewhere in the middle of *Kwabosal*. My mom gets off to undertake the adventure she alone is capable of, buying lots of fresh produce for very little money. We do not know how she does it as we stay in the car drinking sugarcane juice, or fresco with pâtés from Boulangerie Saint Marc that my father brings us from his shorter trips in the surroundings. In addition to these morning adventures, we children will get during the weekends churches and bible camps and more churches and bible camps instead of beef ball stews.

Tomorrow morning, the morning after, and the mornings after that other morning, God willing, I will wake up, help the kids get ready to go to school, or by the lake, or to the library. In our Saint Paul two-bedroom, I will stage before their eyes that life is sound and steady, the fiction they need for now. Frost will show up on the window screens. I will sit down at our kitchen table and add words to empty pages on my computer screen. Those pages, I know, will never pretend to carry the unsteadiness of us. Some days, it will feel like this is my last breath. I can't say whether it's a deliverance or a curse. My battery is dying. Annie and Max will learn to ruminate to save themselves from oblivion. I will force them to ruminate, for the same reason my dad brought all of us to a gathering at the Holiday Inn hotel in the Champ de Mars in Port-au-Prince on a Sunday morning. We were not to forget who we were, so before we knew what was happening, my mom, my dad, and all of us children—and there are six of us, a soccer team in all—stood in front of a sitting crowd and sang:

Rien n'est impossible à Dieu
Il est le même il ne change pas
Rien n'est impossible à Dieu
Ce qu'il a fait il le fera
Et si tu t'approches de lui
Tout changera autour de toi et dans ta vie
Car rien n'est impossible à Dieu (bis).

We found ourselves in Saint Michel this Sunday morning, back on our two feet as we carry our voices with fervor in the Holiday Inn hotel conference room singing *God can do the Impossible*. Our audience travelled happily with us for a few minutes with their hands clapping, their feet hitting the floor, and their shoulders waving left and right, and left and right. For my father, a dream takes short breaks but does not die. We live by faith; things will get better; and our misery is not all that we carry in our suitcases. Then one weekend, we received the news our grandfather passed.

Pèjo lived in Nan Kalvè, Saint Michel. I hold the distant and blurred vision of strolling around his house to find him on his rocking chair. I come up to him, roll and fold and press my fingers over his shaved head to get a *kap*, a crack. I do not have a photograph of him. I carry the lines of his face on the tips of my fingers. My father, on the other hand, wears *Pèjo* on himself, his cells, his name. Now that my own father is 80 years old, he is the face of his own father, and the face of my father is the only photograph I have of *Pèjo*. The death of my grandfather began another kind of departure. I have forgotten how to interlace my fingers together, fold them, and add to my thumb the pressure that lands a *kap*, a crack on the scalp of one's head. My dad sold one by one the family's properties, and my mom got into a nursing school. The dead always make a point of keeping things in order.

2010, Quakes, and Assemblages

I like to think that January 12, 2010, started out in Port-au-Prince like a fine busy Tuesday with the sun standing tall, arms and legs opened and the wind sifting through. Many begin their day with a café-au-lait. At the entrance of their houses, they chat with their neighbors about noises heard the night before or brother Raoul dating one of the neighborhood girls. Did some of them wake up in the morning feeling that this day wouldn't turn out like any other? I imagine many going to work or to school, and so many tap-taps carrying them to their destination read "*L'homme propose, Dieu dispose.*"

The season of crowded bones
January
shuffling around concrete and cars and rubble
epochs turning yellow
skulls
jaw bones
tibias and blue lips
there were a half million of
pigs to crack the plates but
would not expose the maroons

26 seconds
to tear down the walls
layers of buildings to topple each other
giant oak trees to lie on their best
side corpse-like
not pitied and lifeless
the way of
half a million slaughtered some decades ago
300,000 only they count

16:53
what is there to see?
up there a bottle of Balvenie floating in a sea of Miami Rice
poulets-aux-hormones agogo
the stamp of red lips on a bone of Marlboro
stark naked and

standing with *diri Latibonit* laughing their way out
of a bony sea

outbreak à l'infini

There are the people and they are thrown; there are the cities
of the people that are thrown; there is the ground holding the
cities and the people thrown; more than half of million slaughtered; three naval ships; countless overthrows; 16:53: Tuesday,
January12, 2010, is global time; there is the underground quaking beneath the feet of the people thrown; bottles and cans and
pans and ankles chewed and thrown. Frantz Duval throws in
Le Nouvelliste *Les Secondes Qui Ont Tout Changé* and Eyjafjalla-
jökull closes the airspace, its travelers are trapped and thrown;
an explosion of a BP oil drilling rig off the coast of Louisiana;
female suicide bombers detonate bombs in two Moscow subway
stations; there is Katrina; there is Flint, and the invention of
water; Carrefour is shaken under the cries of Hurray, *yo bay li*,
and South Korea is thrown in as the first non-G8 nation to host
a G-20 summit; *We Are the World 25 for Haiti* is released and an
8.8-magnitude earthquake shocks Chile; President René Préval
gives three years to clear up the rubble and 190 South Korean
Peacekeepers throw themselves in Léogâne with Cuba announc-
ing a fifth field hospital; the Minnesota Women's Press releases
What Women Want, my daughter bursts out she wants to be a
gymnast when she grows up. The price of gasoline in Saint Paul
tops $3 a gallon; Clinton orders six warships to waters off Haiti
to enforce the U.N. trade embargo; electricity is finally restored.

My suitcase is a shuffling land, the soil that returns on itself,
opens itself up.

Right after the earthquake I told Max and Annie we're not going
back to Haiti. My daughter was three years of age, my son not yet
one year old. It would comfort me to know that, like my father, I
could start teaching them *vous n'êtes pas n'importe qui*. But who
am I? I do not know. Back in the 1990s it was said that our problem was the language, of being the right skin color, of leaving the
native land, and before that the problem was two men named

Duvalier, and before all that no one knew where the story begins. The dream was to return to Africa. My dream was to make it to the Congo. 2010 became the passage, and it's a lifelong passage for which I selected a small red suitcase with a zipper in the middle to put the three of us in. This is home. It sits in the upper left side of my closet, which I visit once in a while. Each year the zipper stretches itself out with expired passports, classroom pictures piling up, defunct travel permits, expired insurance cards, TPS papers, newspaper sheets yellowing, and others debris like smells of closed dark rooms, pieces of us breaking into pieces we cannot quite assemble back, steams of us disintegrating, ashes of us disappearing. Here it is, our life zipped up. If we have to leave our apartment due to an emergency, all to do is lift myself up, pick up the red suitcase from the upper left side of the closet, and begin again. Though it would be better not to carry any suitcase other than my body which is mostly anyway, vents, memories, and naked bones.

Three times a week, my daughter and I ride Bus-16 down University Avenue on our way to Headstart where she goes to preschool. She and I wait impatiently to get off the bus. As soon as we get off, we hop and skip and tootle and sing *Je suis un artiste et je viens d'Haiti*. In the distance between the bus stop and her day care center she is also learning not to forget *C'est la mère Michelle qui a perdu son chat* or *Panama m tonbe*. On my way back from dropping her off, I walk toward the bus stop with my body somewhere left behind a very long time ago. I sit in the bus alone and think of this poem to write one day about my mom telling her friends the family story of fleeing Saint Michel. In the Bus-16 some twenty years later, it's a lot like being thrown into the edges of another world, into the slit of times made one.

On the computer screen, hundreds of immigrants and refugees are detained at the JFK Airport. Behind the fences, their families await. An overthrow of some sort. Chants, protests, and signs shriek and shout: "Stop Muslim Ban", "We The People", "No ban no wall", "Hands off of my family". But they always had their hands on your family, didn't you know this?

Annie and Max are doing their homework. The day before, they learnt at school *This land is your land*, and they sang it over and over before me camping in the kitchen as if to ask, do you know this song? They do not yet know their history. But which one to pass on? So much happens in the roaming. We get our fruits and veggies at the Keystone food shelf; speak French and Creole at home; wait at the bus stop each morning for the yellow bus that will bring them to school to gather some good jokes on trump and Hillary. On our way back from music lessons on Thursday evenings we will feel like eating a Big Mac. This is all the history upon which they chew, and every now and then my daughter throws in, *Max was born in New York* as if this is it. They have not yet heard about Savann Dezole. They do not know about the Haitian Pig slaughter, nor the uprooting of the Artibonite rice in favor of the Miami rice. The sweat, the smells, the traces, and the effigies made in New York I carried on my back in Rue Tiremasse's corners as if I was the backyard, the shithole. I know that song.

we were thrown to Port-au-Prince
is how Mother tells our story fleeing Saint-Michel
thrown like a stone
uprooted from the land
twenty years later I carry a moun-nan-nò
accent . . . not on purpose
(well not entirely)
I belong to places that never met
(or so they think)

A computer is one more suitcase I carry to stitch with the tips of my fingers, stones and bridges, rivers and seas, and hammocks. In Saint Paul, I reunite with Saint Michel not for its Scott Fitzgerald Theater, its Minnesota State Fair, or a load of yellow *mangoes fransik* marked 'from Haiti' exposed in the Mississippi Market on Selby Ave. It's the fresh deep green grass under my feet; the hummingbirds chirping and the dry maple leaves rustling against each other in Pat and Steve's backyard on hot summer days; it's drinking *Cremas* at my friend Zenzele's with our bare feet taking in the murmurs of the ground. It is above all noticing my daughter's notebook full of Megan Trainor's new hits that will unearth my love affairs with Michel Sardou and

Mireille Matthieu and unleash from my gut *Les Lacs du Conne-mara* and *La Paloma* as if it was yesterday. I didn't know then Sardou's *Si les Ricains n'étaient pas là*. I know it now and I sing very loud in my Saint Paul two-bedroom *if the American wasn't there, many would still be in Germany* and I would still be in Saint-Michel or Port-au-Prince *à saluer je ne sais qui*. The Ricains have always been the ghost we carry on our back; the ghost we chase away like demons; whose spirits we evoke any time we feel like it; the common denominator that we move around with the tips of our fingers. How to explain that this land is your land is a dizzy feeling of inhabiting the other and the self altogether. Eventually, a suitcase will not just sit there, in the upper right side of a closet room. And a small red suitcase of any sort is that special after all and will stitch lands and bony rivers altogether.

The call

I lift the computer off the table, arrange it in its pocket. I am about to call my Dad. I will not set up the terms of the conversation, nor ask him first thing what he ate, where he's been, how's mother. I will talk about home the way I have never done before, how I miss him, and the impossibility to bring the kids for a visit. We are only the memories of us, have no money, no papers, no time, no will, and no getting ourselves in order. I am ready for him to share how he misses me. We will sit with our power-lessness, with our rage and bitterness, and the discontent he and Mother carry in the pit of their stomach that I now carry in the streets of Saint Paul.

Tell me about your exile, Father. How come you did not tell us about the hat you keep in a corner of your bedroom? This hat that covered your eyes and your shoulders when you flew Saint Michel? How do I know? My friend Jude told me. I was shocked he knew about the hat, and I didn't; I was shocked the hat has survived. What else do you have in your suitcase? A pair of old socks? A nail clipper? The names of your horses? Overthrown rivers and memory slits? It's not just the hat that lives in your closet. Tell me about the madness and the fear that took you by hand and pushed you through Port-au-Prince; the way your nails and fingers were fisted and curled into your palm and into each other very hard while you witnessed those searching to kill you stopping the running bus and asking if you were in there. You were in there, behind your hat and sunglasses, they did not know this. Tell me about the paralysis that fueled your veins all the while your heart was pounding whether or not you were going to make it. Did you ever make it? I am hungry for you to tell me how it feels to dwell in a hunger you know will never be assuaged. What happened to my mom's little pink-salmon dress?

Those things we never talk about like leaving home all of a sudden; the starting over; the regrets; the hidden dreams and forgotten lives. I today live my life before the kids as if this is all life is about and wishing this wasn't it all. On alien soil I ruminate over my own suitcases and hidden hat. See? I have learnt to flee my own selves and the languages of my dreams. But today, I carry a suitcase as wide as the Mississippi River, as mad as Savann Dezole.

I cannot wait for our next visit. Summer 2020, God willing. I will pack my suitcase the way one begins learning to write. I envision the clothing, the toothbrushes, the artifacts, and everything else into their slots. Before I start packing I know that the handkerchiefs will go in the upper pocket; several t-shirts will be placed on top of each other; I will fold one-third of the t-shirts' body on the right side towards the center, then fold the sleeves in the opposite direction; and to finish, I will roll the t-shirts together into a ball that will go in one side of the suitcase. The other side is for pants and skirts. In between the different compartments I place shoes and sandals. A bottle of body lotion and a few bar soaps will hold everything else together like braces prevent teeth from being stranded. By the way, Annie is asking for braces; she thinks it's cool. There's no room for snacks nor cracks, everything seems to hold everything else together. But keeping my baggage in symmetry is a vain exercise. In the end, shirts, pants, toothbrushes, and interstices latch to each other and reinvent their space.

How is Mother? I entered 2017 with Nana Mouskouri's "*Quand tu chantes je chante avec toi liberté*", her graduation song. She was carried by the melody, remember? She is wrapped in her floating gown, green or reddish, I do not remember. But the melody flows out of my computer all the time now and I can see her feet sitting gently in a pair of white nursing shoes; she has her lips pursed, she is whistling *Song for Liberty* and maybe, too, our being thrown into Port-au-Prince. How did I get here, she must have thought; was it what she was singing as she was taking her diploma from her nursing school faculty?

So, your mom is a schoolteacher and also a nurse, my son asks as he passes by.

It is with the hope of voyaging at the margin of another world that I retire myself in my worlds, each morning. When I observe a grain of sand among its peers, I have difficulties in singling out a grain among the pile. After all a pile of sand stands out for its togetherness. Each grain is the face of the sand and one grain is also the other. Granules mingle, travel, and rub against each other. At my kitchen table, I ruminate and chew on the edges of merging worlds, because I have the childish wish to journey like a grain of sand, and throw away like a stone, the idea that there is a certain way I should exist in the universe.

Some thirty years ago in Rue Guerrier, those feet floating in a white pair of nursing shoes made the way for our escape through Pastè Lubin's property while our house was being consumed by fire. We made it in the middle of the night through fallen leaves and fresh cut grass as we dragged behind us small bags of tablecloths, linen, and bed sheets. My mom is a runaway too. Throughout the years I have seen the lines of the past within the creases of a few tablecloths and window curtains more than 30 years old. They have survived the fault lines of time with patience and stubbornness. As for the salmon-pink dress, I am content to imagine it lying in my memories, unchanged.

I say goodbye to my father, as my daughter approaches, *you may have the computer now.*

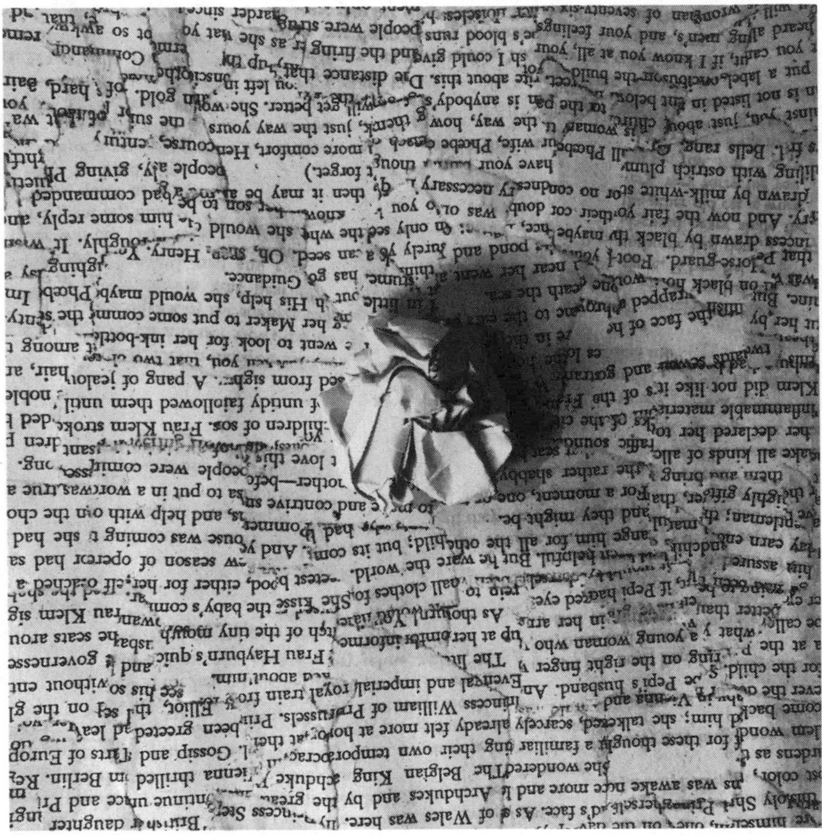

-4-
Ordinary EarthQuakes

a
Aperture

It can begin with
a room
neither big nor small
a ground not yet the place
two legs seeking repose beyond
the ribbons of the Mississippi River
the other side of *Rivyè* Savann Dezole
two waterways sliding back and forth
one threshold to another
unlike how you walk out on an old backyard
a troublesome ocean
a stream of breadcrumbs
all the ground you need
you don't know that
yet
how you sway
the *bitasyon* where the water erodes a childhood
home
payback for having stolen from the cow a gallon of fresh milk
no one drinks anyway anymore
the moment that spills
the great dark river upon which two feet fiddle to meet
Saint Paul wearing the future on its face
just lots of hearsay so far
far away from Savann Dezole
getting in the way
of currents waiting for
two feet walking themselves
out

like a holy ghost

so close and
not yet home
how a trickle moves
swirls and not yet alien
two feet wrapped up in a Carabella blanket dress ready to see
Angelia Tezen breaking free to
hang around a beloved fish fighting
the sway of two waters of
two feet fraying their moment
to face the dead getting closer by the minute
they are the future now
And before the eyes the first snow claiming the ground
It's not fair.
one does not just drop
blend in
then disappear with the composure of a first snowfall
of waterways that mend
the desire to set the clock into the past,
prayer-like

and can-I-choose amnesia
slides off in the uncomfortable waves between a youthful river
eyeing
another.
The savannah:
Just a stain now
filled with malice
hails and plucks and punches
has beginnings and holes and negotiates
any grounds anywhere of
two feet journeying
on the edges of two rivers
of waterways some big some small
of the ground under two feet
of the feast of the dead
of the waves of two *rivyè* meeting
to not forget where it begins

an old backyard
the turmoil of a troublesome ocean
a trail of breadcrumbs
the home the moment you dream
to way
to know.

b
Beginning again

b as in boy, e as in egg, a as in apple, u as in university, d as in dog,
e as in egg again, l as in laugh, a as in apple, i as in internet, n as
in no, and e as in earthquake.

God, they say, proceeds without saying so.

There were thousands of reasons why I would stand up in the
middle of the road wholly naked with an unfinished monologue.
A home has rooms in the ordinariness of things, of thought, void,
matter, the blank page; in the breathing space between one event
and the next and beyond; in the void between one world and another not yet here, not yet alien, not yet fashioned. To find myself
in the business of spelling names over the phone, every day, in
every way, in every breath, is the proof that there is nothing ordinary about starting over; I mean the breathing two apparently
stranded commas bring along.

That must be the reason why I will not get used to saying
my name in a no language that is a no home. I spell my name
to spell myself. I pour out each letter with great economy of
junction, voice, breath, breadth, and with the throat soaking and
gripping and sending life off into all possible and unimaginable
directions. How can one give themselves to another language, to
another home without displacing their gut structure? A breathing space between two fault lines, two commas, and in-between
no ground, no grammar, no geographies is the manner I get used
to a refrain that bites. A breathing utterance is the gap between
the before last and the never ultimate last quake that goes out
within the gentle inflection of an empty space. Home after all
has the skeleton of the status quo. A sauntering comma makes always a point, brings together incompatibles that seem seamless.

L'homme propose.

I will not live one more day without spelling names. Every

day I spell: transitional housing, food assistance, health insurance, a quarter of a gallon of milk, and many other things you will not spell out if you are not voyaging in between stranded commas; in between one halt and the other, and the next, and beyond, and beyond the beyond; endless halts, routes, shifts, and nuances you could learn quickly eagerly to earn the right to start over, and start over after each comma that is not a semicolon. The kids also return to their alphabet and grammar lessons. Like a stain we learn even more quickly but not eagerly that starting over does not give you the privilege to call home the place to which your feet could be welded for a very long time. We start over anyway, without the unflickering finality of the period.

Yes, this is my phone number.

In the living room, I go from walking to jumping and to running and to no breathing for a piece of paper and a pen to write down the miracle of the day, a tunnel to breathe through with my head buried momentarily under the sand, the subtle breath between two commas. I should now empty my lungs now.

I am from Haiti, I am a student at the University Of Minnesota Humphrey Institute Of Public Affairs, My kids arrived here two weeks before the earthquake, We were not planning to stay here and our plan has changed since, yes . . . it was a blessing.

I nailed it. Okay. But it's like spitting out I am not your typical beggar. My commas here are a matter of aesthetics with the poise of the pompous snow who could disappear anytime they want. Over time, the tremor travelling at the tips of the fingers is to learn that the space between two commas is the perimeter ground on which the two feet stand, that in-between these two commas, fault-line-like, you take your losses under your armpits with the slowness moving from one tragedy to another allows. You do not go any further nor faster. An earthquake does not have the normal spin of the ground that suddenly opens and trembles at will and with whom you do not tremble, not yet. In between two commas, a resting place, a home.

Can you give me the address please?

The person on the other line that is not a stranded comma has just what I need, knows where to find a gallon of milk. Commas are like a home, a pause, a repose, and will lift anyone who journeys in the shade of their stains.

How do you spell it please?

A stain will call out other stains who fault to know they are just that, stains. You'll learn to go on with just the ground under your feet or with the space between two rivers. And you bring between two commas a semicolon here and there while sneaking and screwing and being screwed like any stain lingering on a fabric, surprisingly gentle, daringly feisty, and with poise. Home is a matter of care.

Between January 12, 2010, and January 12, 2011, and the next spacing, and the next quake, and the next chapter to come, one after the other, back-to-back, in empty spaces only the mending heart notices the parallel slit, the wholeness in the brokenness, the unfinished monologue in inflection, in thread, in diffraction, in void, in emptiness; a scratch almost-like, a spin, a flicker on a clean plate; in two commas spacing; the way the earth catches with itself in between breadths.

c

Chocolate Cake

Like the painter who struggles over their subject matter through geometric abstractions rivers and trees and glowing lights and sees themselves through seas and skies, some ponder over what to paint for the last show, the final song that will resume decades of lifelong struggles and feats and feasts. One is so much more than a masterpiece behind its veil. Every teardrop, each time a finger moves, each line of the face, is a revelation, a constellation, a moment, a spark. And many hunt for the most suitable emplacement, the proper tile, and wonder whether the canvas should be black or white or brown or in marble. They won the bet, and they know this long before their rotten cold meat enters the stage. They have already decided whether the chosen casket is worthy enough and learned in the process the world's tiniest things are its biggest, themselves, period.

Eventually, they hint at their kin the lines of the poem to be written on the tombstone, the letter font, and how large it ought to be. Family members, friends and daughters who have accompanied them at school graduations, marriages, funerals, and many more who have shared their beds, their sweat, their meals learn in the process the kind of marvel the earth carries.

When the time comes, they will pull off the right epitaph their ones deserve for knowing them so well, not because they were told so. They are all in this together. Though many do not know when their light will hit, some live long enough to concede it's okay to deliver the last act with a dust of feverishness whenever it strikes. To some extent the wealthy and the healthy and the lucky will prepare their departure, and exit the stage graciously for their last home. This—is a tour de force.

And many more prepare their last home but not like the raven who does nothing without assessment. They walk out, sometimes to buy, sometimes to sell, and sometimes to stare at the steak they are saving for. To church they go sometimes to not give their souls to sinking ship, and sometimes at the clouds they gaze to stop the rain, then to poking hails they sometimes offer their naked heads. They walk in to miss the train after getting off at the last train station. They run, they rain, they let the water overflow. They forget to pick up the bread, then eat the bread they have not picked up at the bakery. Sometimes they tell, sometimes they mute.

Life is a roller coaster of kids graduating, marrying, and disappearing; of neighbors birthing, communing, singing, and dying; of riding up tap-taps every day to the hills of Pilbowo and to the streets in downtown; of working as discharger *anbalavil* and making sure the fresco is well sold under the sun. It is an art not to get into the business of preparing the last song but of living it in every drop and by the second through the sometimes, the every-days, and not in the what-ifs, the what-will-bes, and what-could-bes. It will happen and, no mistake, they take care of it. The final show is not of a lesser chef d'oeuvre, is it?

An earthquake is a chocolate cake shaped island that mixes everything up: the lines of the river with the cracks of the trees and with the ashes of bones, chewed bones, chewed ankles and everything else, those who paint their last song and many others who don't and steal from all the right to contract their last masterpiece.

d
De l'égalité des races humaines

1888 (three years before that): Anténor Firmin publishes *De l'*égalité des races humaines challenging Gobineau's guesses on black inferiority, brain sizes, and englishmen as measures of human intelligence. We're in the boat right from the start, we can't flee anywhere. We sew, we stitch, and we continue to fiddle the fault lines.

2018 (fast afterward): The scholar of queer people of color is now the director of the Studies Plot Area Thing. To get an appointment, you pass through her bondwoman, a cheerful white young very really young lady who profusely diligently serves the used-to-be-oppressed-and-colonized-and-slave-and-now-serving-as-a-slave-owner who will not show up to her appointments. The newly appointed slave owner is too busy and her slave too happy demonstrating that white people can stay happily in bondage. More than a century after Firmin everyone is dutifully redressing, owning, and shareholding the lines and plots of history.

e
Earthquake

This is me telling the kids about Granny.

Granny rocks her rocking chair on the veranda of her house. The grey warm air of the night descends upon her back, blends with her sighs, her voice, her breath. We children camp around her large *moumou* under the light of a small *tèt gridap*.

Granny tells stories to heal, to silence the way her teeth, only what is left of them, jangle in her mouth as if to break loose from the turbulences her frail body won't disclose; the things she endured throughout years of hungers and wars and expeditions, like living soaked then dried up to the bones each day, being born one day to die the next, and being born again and dying afresh at every day cycle. The truths of our lives never make their way into history books, Granny says. She joins her palms together each time she tells, each time she rocks. In each moment her finger bones juggle, twine into one another, then spread out in hurry; her fingers battle their own battles, they are not a piece of cloth you cut out and toss away.

We sit on the ground around Granny and receive the words, the breathings, the signs, the spits, and pieces of Granny's organs one by one: liver, brain cells, lungs, blood, and other body parts and pieces. The light from the *tèt gridap* goes off but never completely as the wind flips and flops. Here we are with stories unfolding before our eyes like the light swinging and going in circle, then fading and coming back again. Some stories make the wind wander; others pull themselves from under the rubble.

There are millions of earthquakes stories the flame of a *tèt gridap* will hold without going too bright or completely off. Our eyes swing and follow the flow of Granny's eruption. We nod. *Goudou goudou* was one quake among many. Granny tells about thousands of Haitians butchered some decades ago in Sendomeng because their tongues refuse the rock and roll of a proper *perijil*. She stomps her feet and her fingers go click and clack and click and clack as she recounts bodies beaten, tortured, and pushed to death on the cold floors of Casernes Dessalines and Fort-Dimanche during the Duvalier years. She spits the stories one after the other and the flame of the *tèt gridap* shivers, then stands still.

Granny knew about two brothers given to death with tires in flame glued around their chests in the street of Delmas 18 where she lived. Granny knew of a body of her own that died decades ago among piles of other bodies tortured, raped, and piled on top of each other in the same street where the two brothers were burnt. A body raped and left to death never comes back. Under the light of the *tèt gridap*, our Granny died a long time ago.

Every night, Granny's corpse sobs, cries, and outbursts over little children going weeks without food and making their beds out of empty stomachs bloated like a balloon. A doctor would open their bodies, Granny says, all they would find is dirt and dirt and clay and paste and vent. This is a *goudou goudou*. January 12, 2010, was not the quake of the century. Granny swings, and she swings back and forth and very hard she rocks her chair against the wind; she is mad; this is her, pushing away oblivion and mass killings and ordinary quakes. *Fòk nou pa bliye.*

Every night our feet take big steps, and our fingers swing and battle against the wind under the light of the *tèt gridap*. We rock our bottoms on the ground with our hearts travelling back and forth and propelling our breaths all over the flame of Granny's lamp. We nod over our dead bodies, over our light fragile and fading for having gone through carnages, death squads, tsunamis, rapes, rubble, and erasures every time the sun shows up. We tell about 9/11 and children drinking poisoned water in Flint. We wobble against everyday death, everyday rape, everyday war, and everyday hunger here and every where.

Almost at the end of each *lodyans*, and no one knows exactly when, Granny would stand on her two feet all of a sudden. It's one more swing to the wind as she brings around her waist the folds of her dress, as her eyes grow bigger. Then Granny spits, what the hell children, shake it off, our biggest quake, and she yells and keeps yelling louder and louder, it's our amnesia, our dumbness, we go as if we don't know who quake and shake us all, who starve us to death, and who kill and who profit from our killings, from our deaths, from our rapes, from our starvation, this is the real earthquake. Then suddenly, like it all began, she lets go of her dress and returns to her seat that she rocks and rocks and swings. She hits the wind. Granny rocks. Each swing and each hit and each rock was the story of another quake, of another rubble, of another truth to remember under the light of the *tèt gridap*.

f
Fucked up

I am fucked up. There's no exit, no path, no lights ahead, no prospects of surviving the current order of things, no dreams after which to run. After having tried to make it, run after the dream, and persisted, there must be a way, a path, an exit someway somehow some time to come, I am relieved, there's no exit. There's no making it, no dream, no light to come, no tomorrow. This is the thrill of disenchantment. It puts you naked up to the bones, and nothing matters enough to cover up a bare life. My nakedness is my liberation, I am fucked up, and I need nothing here.

g
Goodwill

It's been more than two weeks. I am hungry for your voice. I will not call to gasp your breath that could put me to sleep, I will not subdue this thirst, this hunger, all of me drenched, torn, angry, and free. I am trapped. There's no escape to ease the guilt and the shame, the load of a lifetime now, for staying away, for not calling, for not visiting, for leaving behind my mom hungry of me, for having overcome my hunger of you.

I am now at a Saint Paul Goodwill store where I sometimes carry my load of anxiety, torment, and undesirable hungers. Today again, I am walking in between mounted clothing walls asking myself whether the lines of your face have multiplied, and your jaws settled deeper into your cheekbones. I miss you. What's my mom been up to lately? Did she go to the doctor? I would like to call one day and hear that everything is great, you don't need me, I can stay away for as long as I want to. But my hunger of you is more than I can contain. I live it every day, unbridled. And I will call. I will call and ask how you're doing, about the church service last Sunday, what you've eaten in the morning, questions you know that come out of each stranded call. This refrain is how I suppress the guilt, the shame, my unquenchable hunger of you. After the call I suppose I will go on with my life fully loaded with the day to day, but empty of you. I am dying. Are your shoulders still up high?

Here we are, over the phone, talking to each other about churchgoers, about kids, about Mother who's doing better after her last visit at the doctor. You know I know I will not let the conversation slip away. I will not face the real wounds, being locked up, and not being able to do anything about being locked up. You won't, either. But at least you sigh and you let slide at each sigh the impossibility to say things that cannot be said with an ocean in between. *De je kontre manti kabba.* We are doing a pretty good job not voicing to each other the things we know we cannot do anything about. We've learned, how powerless we are.

But all of a sudden, you dropped things off, all of it. Today I see you like the jumper, unsure during the takeoff, but gradually holding the space and the game within their body at the angle of their choice while walking then running and then speeding towards the bar. I am out of breath, I gasp, I drift. I am in disarray. I guess you've leaned on the strength built up during the raking and the ploughing, in the voids between one call and the next, in the spacings between our silences. You've measured, I suppose, the distance between your backyard and the wall behind which I stand. Your angle of 45 degrees is perfect, you raised yourself up in the air, and dropped your weight, and not all of it, on your two feet on the other side of the ocean. How about I come home? A few minutes before your jump, I was just sauntering between the aisles of a Goodwill mall, unconcerned.

The worst is to realize you could sense how hard living away is on me and how harder it is to not talk about it. As hard as it is I don't know what to say. I have to go. On a red Goodwill sofa in Saint Paul, I am sinking, this isn't happening.

I will call my friend Lily. For a moment, I will switch up your voice for my friend's ears to clear up my mind. This is it! All the while I was running, Goodwill shopping, hungering, and sleeping at night with both eyes closed after feeding the kids Granny's stories or those of Tonton Bouki and Ti Malice, I did not know what the hell I was doing in the land of Tonton Sam. Now I know. I cannot go home.

I would need to search for a an on-site partner first, a body-guard, a soldier. The kind of thing a wedded woman has that says to neighbors, uncles, and other males *mal intiontionés*, stay away from my property, you will not open her door at night, walk into her bedroom and fuck her and her kids; the kind of thing that warns passersby, *zenglendoes*, and *kadejakès*, you will not pull her in the bushes while she walks alone in her neighborhood at 6:00 pm so you can point a gun at her. The kind of thing many tied-down women are cemented to and forced to put up with no matter how painful and abusive coupling up under the law and under the divine protection may be. Is all this, ransom for living guarded against external killings and outdoor rapes? I will not come home.

"Pour le pays mourir est beau" has a sudden bitter taste, Father; this is what I would like to tell you, but will not. My so-called-pays has not protected me against the brothers, the uncles, against *les maris* and the neighbors. *Salut!*

h
Handwriting

I brought the sheet to my nose. This encounter with the subtle-ties of a sheet of paper jolted across oceans, lands, and across vents is not what it seems like. A soft green color paper that survived the crossing of continents, storms, slave ships, and the master's bedroom is all you need to relive Christopher Colum-bus sailing across La Pinta, La Niña, and La Santa Maria to collect unwanted wombs.

You tap a finger against the sheet to feel the echo of waves hitting themselves against the deck of a slave ship, raindrops yearning on a metal roof, or a wrinkled golden leaf you will not bring to the slave traders and their cargoes. It is a fleeting smell; a silent eruption; a glint of living on borrowed time. A stain reposes itself in the middle of the sheet and hits you like a tap on a drumhead. Maybe the remains of a café-au-lait spilled centuries ago, ghosts of coffee and sugar canes, waves in turbulences.

The handwriting is delicate, elegant, and stylish. The writer must have found pleasure travelling and crossing their fingers and their senses on the paper. A fine line cuts the paper in half lengthwise. The first word reads: monsieur. The letter M, larger and bigger than the others, would be the equivalent of today's Lucida sophisticated M. There is the coffee, the sugar, the cracks of the whip, and an Okpoho-type manilla from southeastern Nigeria that repeat themselves throughout. In assemblage.

A soft green color paper serving as a financial letter report written by Fourgassie to Milhau. One lives in the France metropole; the other manages the canefields in the colony of Saint-Domingue, plus the slaves in their domains. Your senses reach out subtly to those at the bottom of the sea who haven't made it at the shore of the Cap Français but whose void dominate the vacuum, and millions more who reached the harbor and whose odors and heavy groans and stifled cries survived on a sheet of paper laying in the Bell Library archives on another side of the Atlantic.

The first sentence reads *"Je reçois par la flotte nouvellement arrivée au Cap les lettres du premier Juillet au mois de Novembre 1781"*. It has taken four months for the letter to find its destination. But a letter has no destination. But a letter is a destination. But a letter holds many lives and traces and senses and smells; smells of open boat; traces of negroes' blood and dead girls body parts; and geographies of sugarcanes and golds. But a letter flocks and assembles. And there's the smell of the unknown and the wave of the deep a letter attuned to all holds, brings to the nostrils, smells of unceasing births, of wombs crossing, of wombs to come.

A soft green color paper who holds so suddenly the too familiar rancid and bitter smell of my parents' bedroom during days of rain and closing doors. Annie and Max will write letters to Grandpa and Grandma with their own Lucida handwritings. A piece of paper may very well serve as routes for the smells, the senses, and the odors of times and things that are never so far away, the passage from one to many and their crossings. This is the kind of encounter that can happen when a paper of shit reaches the brain, the fingers, and the senses; one finds that a shit is a sheet, a ship, a hold, an open boat to the cracks of times, to the things disjointed and sensed here and there, not yet a disappearing, a hold deep and subtle.

i
In-betweenness is

the moment the old backyard gets in the way turning home a lot like a distant star so close and so unreachable; the knock-knock-who's-there game you play anywhere you ground a red suitcase where you store the traces and the lines you no longer recall, the forgotten accents, the unwanted breasts, the bland jokes, and the name that is your childhood home no one here ever heard of; the moment you open up the folders, the notebooks, the picture albums, the ashes of you trying to get yourself right; the interstice in the split second you notice in your suitcase lids in-between spaces in-between times in-between lands and in-between holes another you growing closer, unreachable and boundless as if getting hold of yourself was the impossible dream.

j
Janil 1957–2010

The question is how to recollect with those who fought the fight we wish could have been ours if the stars were spookier, subtler, or covered with a tint of weirdness. People we've known from near and then from far and then we get dissolution for distance in trade-offs. But it's never a fair give and take, for what will close the deal is distance sailing like a messenger and bringing the feel of death to one's palate. How to remember is a gut-wrenching twist. We search in our memories for the lines of the face, for this part of the cheek that lies down, tender, soft, and immortal; lines we have touched with our lips, with our fingers; those parts that have become us and now cold and rigid, a star so close, so far, so distant. You then begin to dwell on the light of their palms, flashlight-like, and wish you could have known how to live closer to their fire.

To realize you will never get this chance in between remote stars makes you sad and melancholic, enough to curse the place, the morning coffee, the politics, the bad circumstances. But not enough—you are thinking ashamed of yourself and afraid of your own cowardice—to want to throw in the towel. At best, you mourn for a few days, a month, or for even a year. You agree with yourself you will be haunted for years to come in the midst of many things like taking care of kids and the everyday that does not give you time to learn how to remember proper. The question is how to recollect with those who have turned up the light in our darkness.

Some say Anil's death has called the deaths of more than 300,000 the afternoon of January 12, 2010. Four hours after men on motorcycles gunned him down the earth trembled. Holy shit, death is contagious, nature is seeking revenge. You still don't know how to mourn, so the voice in your head, hungry for solace, hopes that those who committed the deed are dead by now. How can you know for sure? Dogs on motorcycles fly fast and they may just have escaped in another town or at the DR border. Now you're screaming? What kind of revenge is that? Life is not fair? There's no point about rambling on the dead; no recipe for even how to grieve 300,000 in cash or trade millions more in kind.

And you and I and you and I, trapped in recollection stunts, are now recomposing the physiology of stars in the midst of everyday quakes and everyday trade-offs supposedly equal. A deal has no closure. There is a way in which, alive and dead, we lay boundless in each other's lives, in each other's souls, in each other's stars, in yours and in mine. We are ghosts to each other; ghosts to those we live in the shadows, spooky and subtle and weird, stars taking turns.

k
knitting
The kids lost the car keys, we have a lot in common, I will not go to the grocery store for tomorrow's breakfast, walls are necessary, it's one hundred degrees outside, you get the president who uses

his face to cover your soul, somehow you can shit exposed and not escape from shit, you are still under cover, the woman was saying to the other woman let me hold your hands so you can cross, my throat itches inside out, shit moves are so gargantuan, the international missionary worker needs an appointment, a friendship is dreamy and hesitant and full of conflicting ideas, we are two weeks old in our place, they should impeach their soul and nothing else, they say I should run wild I don't want to run wild, no spare keys, there is that email to send to the landlord, I wonder what it would be like to spend a year without reading anything any book, I need a bed, the laundry card is not working, ordinary things to write about like coffee or avocado toast or aging, trumping is an historical necessity, we don't have couches to couch, at the bottom of my email signature I write sister I am dying, nor a rocking chair that rocks, I have $1.84 in my bank account, I am going to undertake a pilgrimage I will see no people, I will text my friend I can't meet for coffee, so what if you are forced to uncover bondages passing for democracy, I need to call my mom back, I like it when you touch my hair tell me how pretty I am or that you like my accent, there is a lump growing bigger in my left breast, my sister wrote Tonton Fito is dead, Max has his appointment with the ophthalmologist on Tuesday, I live on a different time each time, Annie's screaming all my clothes are dirty can we go to the laundromat, I need a dream, and Annie gives Max a mohawk haircut, I wanted to say it's not about the money, I worry about my mom's foot pain, I wanted to disagree to bite and get bitten like lovers fight and make up, instead I can't find the comb, they are all nice all smiley all the time, the deadline to renew our health insurance is tonight, I am out of time, I am angry, let's have the fight and not pretend it's all alright tonight, I am family, by now I have missed the food shelf appointment, I am hungry, I thought you were my friend and I just got my personal social worker, I am okay if you can't say the proper thing, who is doing the dishes today, I can't find my shoe, there is a garage sale tomorrow, give me the chance to be your equal, I hear a knock knock at the door, here' a grown-up who can't handle a good fight, did you charge the phone, the wall that transitions you from one side to another, I can't answer the door, I must say something, I can't believe I should explain I didn't vote for DéTé, no one wants to take their shit off and hold it before them, to shit is to take shit . . .

I
Latalay (Sen Michel)

In the picture my sister Eslie stands between a coconut tree and my father's dark green Jeep. Her head is tilted, her eyes are wise and knowing, her air of sophistication. The school uniform is a short-sleeve white t-shirt resting under a light gray dress that falls at the bottom of her knees. Her feet in a pair of shiny black shoes are running away. She goes to school at Coeur Immaculée de Marie. The ease of uncertainty you feel from your sigh and not from the jaded elegance of time slipping off of its time zone. My sister must have worn the uniform only for the occasional picture during a family visit. All Saint-Michel stands in the background.

The ground that returns on itself. Sen Michèl Latalay. Sen Michèl breaking-apart-entangling-returning into multiplicities. A shuffling breathing. The palm of your hand touching itself. The echoes and the voices calling, shaking the abyss. Saint Michel de l'Attalaye opening itself up. A refuge for the less than humans, the maroons, the civilized, the cattle. San Miguel Atalaya churned up, broken apart, exploded, opened up, diffracted and disputed and glued back together and diffracted afresh. Sen Michèl diaspora. Sen Michèl St. Domingue. Saint Michel Saint Paul. Rue Guerrier nan Sen Michèl. Sen Michèl diffused. Sen Michèl womb labor. Womb cattle. Womb sprouting new worlds. To the highest bidder! Sen Michèl Latalay, skins ripped apart, scarred backs, smashed flesh, and broken bones and tortured souls. Blood deep earthing the ground. Ground shaking under the echoes of squalling negroes; under runaway feet; ground quaking, ground touching themselves, ground releasing their guts. Sen Michèl unleashing worlds. And the ground as murmur. Sen Michel excessively murmurs, uncontained, out of geography. Sen Michèl, Sen Michèl Latalay.

The Jeep before our eyes is all yellow and bright. We snap another picture of the car as we cross the Mississippi River bridge. My daughter says her first car will be a Jeep. I hold on tight. I am accustomed to rehearse, my father's first car was a Jeep. My big sister when she was little planted a coconut tree in Saint-Michel's backyard. As my sister's tree grows she would grow, she would continue growing beyond trees and beyond sizes.

m
mardi

It's January, and already gone and cold as we cross the Mississippi Bridge. It's 4:00 pm in Saint Paul the time right before the world snatches itself off from angry currents. We are returning from Eagle Nest with P and S, and the sweat on my back warms on and off as I sit in the gray Ford. Sometimes I tell myself I now know too much to confuse the edge of the east side of the Mississippi River in Minneapolis to its Saint Paul north side or to its faraway Savann Dezole corners. We're heading back home anyway.

Anil was just killed. I have the suspicion that it was during the moment we carried ourselves safe and giving in the underground of the eagle nest. It must have been warm and sweaty in Port-au-Prince and suddenly icy and cold and dry. I am now afraid home is a no place, that the crossing was neither in Minneapolis nor in Saint-Paul nor in Savann Dezole. All this happened from afar, from distant times, from unknown selves and interstices. Who truly can say the earth ever made a comeback?

The day before our trip to Eagle Nest, S emailed they will pick us up. We will ride together underneath where the playground is warmly guarded against walled ices of fault lines, where you can know with precision the temperature thousands of miles away, digest a bombing attempt in Moscow while eating a cheese pizza, or predict the next in line for the guillotine without one hair over your head moving right or left. On our way to Eagle Nest late in the morning of the cold day, Annie chanted like all the times we drive over the Mississippi bridge M-I-S-S-I-S-S-I-P-P-I. That same river we drove over back and forth the whole afternoon and whose waves inside us we were trying to slow down, decelerate, stop from moving. On our way back home, the Mississippi was not the Mississippi anymore at least for me who feels it stirring itself up against the back of my t-shirt and suddenly drying up. We crossed the bridge. We do. Annie M-I-S-S-I-S-S-I-P-P-Ies again.

It wasn't less cold at home nor timeless when P calls, gives me the call of the earthquake of January 12, 2010, in Port-au-Prince, a Mardi at 4:20 or 4:30 or 4:50. Frankétienne who does

not go through time untouched was cooking up in the underground of his house a play about a *tremblement de terre* to come,
the same interstice, the same goudougoudou. I imagine eight
years old girls screaming and shouting and pulling brothers, fathers, aunties, and sisters from under the rubble; a remote leg
turning the center of the earth and circumferencing itself along,
untold final goodbyes, corpse rising themselves in cathedral. In
truth it is a slice of time removed, taken from the subconscious,
from the calendar year, from an epoch I cannot imagine. Who
can say what happened?

A frightened Mardi afternoon, not even a Lundi, of the tragedy of January 12, 2010, at 4:20. *Vingt-six* seconds is all it takes
for the ground to return on itself as we keep time on its toes in
a gray Ford crossing the Mississippi River bridge and rolling like
the old dark green Jeep of my father.

n
nasyon

My story, at least for now, is a few selected lines purposefully ar-
ranged and clogged and choked up in a succession of knots and
pockets and silences, the male, his name, his family, his neighborhood, his nation, his world. I will explode the assemblage.

o
osselets

This was supposed to be about girls juggling *osselet*s on a fine
Tuesday afternoon while listening to Zenglen's last hit on radio
Caraïbes. We sing *Nap peye bill.* Our toes tap the floor; our fingers bulge out; the world is ours for us to sing. Announcements
from the American Embassy would pop out of nowhere to advise their people to leave the country. We are at war. And we crack
up over the tales of wars like all the million times we've heard
these commercials. There are four of us on the ground with our
backs slightly bent forward, our legs open on the floor, and our
heads in tune with the movement of the *osselets* going up and
down and up and down. Our bodies do not sway.

This was supposed to be about each of us taking turn, cheer-
ing, and whistling each time a player lays down their game,
throws in the air an *osselet* the second after, and in half of the

other second right after that, chicka chicka boom boom, turns each of the lying bones on *do* and *cre* and *i* and *s* one after the other nonstop, swipe them all together from the ground while catching up in their palm the last bone arriving from the ceiling. It would be, at some point, my turn to take off with the *osselets*. A pirouette I execute on my bottom, wiggle and jiggle with arms, shoulders, and legs opened up in a confessional moment, then I sweep and strike from the ground all my *osselets* while receiving the travelling bone in the palm of my hand, game on! My war.

This was supposed to be our showing off, our swinging around with our bottoms laying on the ground naked and breathing through our pores, holes, and bones, the cool of the ground underneath. We do not know what Americans look like anyway. Maybe they live in a tower that protects them against *diri Latibonit*, *poul peyi*, and Haitian pigs. Of course, this is a joke. They come for the rice, the land under our derrieres, the chickens, the pigs, and most of all for our shit. In exchange, we get Miami rice, *poul pèpè*, plastic water bottles, and good governance. I am kidding you. Strange that one would be at war with *kochon kreyòl*, *diri Latibonit*, and *poul peyi*. It's hard to teach girls to sing their names.

This was supposed to be about the dirt that slips off our fingers while turning the *osselets* on *do*, on *cre*, on *i*, and on *s* alongside our uncles and brothers playing dominoes under the shade of oak trees. They go around a party of domino screaming *dekabès*. They make the tables scream and tremble at the stomp of their hands. They have several clothespins attached to their jaws and lined in a U shape which make them look like freaky monsters. We do not send them to hell, nor ask them what kind of deal they have with clothespins or with Uncle Sam. There must be some kind of magic in playing dominoes with clothespins pinching jaws. We are not going to declare war on clothespins. We are not going to bring them our own clothespins.

This was supposed to be about girls going on naked and running and chasing each other with water hoses in their hands, splashing water everywhere and turning the sun on its axis. They clear up their throat hum hum hum and stand like a palm tree entirely naked with their legs wide open in the streets, in downtown, or down on the beach. This was supposed to be about that, and about a million of other things like picking up the smoked herrings and the garlic and the charcoal in the street market, or trading *Nap peye bill* for *La isla bonita*. It has never been about that and that and that, that Tuesday afternoon of January 12, 2010. For whatever it's been about, the game goes on.

p
pigs

Christopher Columbus planted a cross in Môle Saint-Nicolas. From Genoa to Hispaniola to Spain it's hard to tell if the trail a dragged suitcase leaves on the ground hints to a home, a place, a geography, or whether there will be bread and chocolate. If my suitcase's upper pocket contains a letter of invitation to a New York City retreat, does this mean I go around wearing my soul like a borrowed skirt. Strange that in the same upper pocket of the same suitcase there could be folded shorts, pants, piles of socks, a forest-green coat, manila in cash, and a collection of vintage 1960s little green, brown, and yellow Marx Plastic US Army Military figurines. A wolf has millions of faces and is thought to enjoy the hunt. There you have half a million pigs slaughtered in the '80s for the result to come out in 2010. Grownups spill. Archive from the Greek, Arkheion, residence of those who command. The Youwès negotiates a naval station in Mole Saint-Nicolas to penetrate the walls they're confused about. If *devlopman* could be exported at a fair price, Miami rice, arsenic chicken, US army soldiers, and pigs and beefs fabricated in the Youwèse would not be granted asylum on Haitian lands. How about we put modern-day Columbus on trial and build a wall for things like *poul pèpè*, Arkansas rice, and *imanitè*?

q
quaking

is to follow the traces of faults lining and voyaging; sometimes overlapping, other times discontinuous; the kachkachlagoliben game they play; mud volcanoes, enndjiwos, earthquakes, humanitarian rescues, cholera outbreak, backpacking, flagging, bible studies, ministah, missionary missions, democracy exchange orders, red-crossings that entertain, carve, swallow, wave, move things around and leave the more or less than humans wondering to whom they owe their roaming and quake and outburst; and how they laugh their way out but lying low like the memory of a forgotten song.

r
restavèk

Let's play a game, will you?
Do you still say my name? Like you used to?
Remember?

You stand straight up early morning in the corner of Kafou Ica, you raise yourself up, you're on your toes, heels upright, you're a statue of yourself, suddenly tall and frightening as hell, you're about to open yourself up, all of you; the passerby doesn't know what's boiling.

At the early dawn I would go and sit with the *machann kafe*, *chofe dife* after sweeping and mopping and after leaving all the house's jars filled of water, but it's never enough to sweep, mop, and bring the water home, so you open yourself up every morning, straight and tall in the corner of Kafou Ica, you contract your chest, lunge forward, your hands you pull behind, and your back, and your fists that squeeze the morning air very tight, for the passerby, one more going mad.

Did you wake up the day after distraught? did you walk towards the corner of Kafou Ica at the dawn and shake the entire neighborhood and yell and scream
tififi vini pale w!!?

The *machann kafe* and I would crack up 'til our gut got mad and I would leave my coffee with the *machann kafe*, to clean up your shoes and the table and the rest of everything else, the early sweeping and mopping and watering were not enough.

Did you say my name after the tremor and wait for me to show up to sweep and mop and clean up your shoes and your underground with my breath my breadth spitting out café-au-lait stirred up in *pen-a-manba*?

The *machann kafe* is under the rubble cracking up with me. *Mi-sye a anba nou*, his hands are tied, will you say my name again, will you crack me up one more time, will you give me another shot, another day to live?

s
storying

Here's the quake story to tell the *descendantes*; and tell it the times they would have become so overused that all they are left with is their song for them to chew over, the times they would have become enlightened enough to carry their mothers' names or no names; or so angry and so bold they call themselves moth-erfuckers.

I have lived with the abuse, the extortion, and the injustices for years. It was not Okay. I dwelled in it. I lived it. I was not Okay but one is not Okay alone. One does not break their chains alone. One is not themselves alone. One is the other. One is many others, like their religion and their mothers and faraway fathers teaching them compliance; their country giving them national-ism over justice; their comrades pushing them lovingly to make things work no matter what. And you are all the time confound-ed and confused and you don't know what it is to make work no matter what; maybe it's taking care of the consort, feeding the household, putting an entire country together, how about nur-turing your own abuse?

And you feed your abuse. You will not settle. You do not know how to get out. You are hungry for something else and you don't know what it is that you are hungry for. So you stay. You stay discontent and patient, alive and numb, still and agitated. Some days, and because you need a reason to keep up with the shit, you go on like the unbridled horse who endures silently and proudly the abuse, the subjugation, the price that will make you a *fanm vanyan*. You go on. You still don't know if you will live long enough to receive the title of the *Fanm Vanyan* Empire Or-der, for it is at the cost of your last drop, your last sweat, your blood clot, all of it spilled and dried up and clogged up inside out and in between. Sometimes, very quickly you get over your-self, aren't you better off than many. In silence, you continue the ploughing and the opening up of what it is you are looking for but do not know what it looks like. Or where to find it.

There is no way out when the center posts of a woman's womanhood ask them to stuff up their voices with dust, with shit, with silences. This is love. Then you tell the friends and sisters you are going to let go. They say you cannot let go. They are in the boat and sinking like the captain with its entire cargo. Besides, they have gotten used to shit, and letting go is not part of the divine. But when the shit lives under your nose, you know what shit tastes like. You know what piles of shit amount to. One more day to stay is one more bull of shit to slug straight back. And another day to stay, you find yourself staying longer and longer for piles of shit turning you into something else, shit, until the moment comes and you can no longer count all the times you want to vomit out both shit and yourself.

There are also neighbor Jean's inconveniences. He whistles every time I walk down the street. He sits all day at the entrance of his house to hunt after the legs, the lips, and the boobs of girls passing by. Neighbor Jean never misses the occasion to track down my lips he says he would like to kiss and shout after me when I walk too fast how come I am so beautiful, why I walk so fast, how I have an attitude. Every day you stumble upon thousands of girl-watchers snarling their teeth like neighbor Jean who smells and feels a girl's arrival before others see them. It's not like I've never felt the everyday hassle, the lawful harassment, the stalking.

A moment comes to you, 2010, and you strike back. Your time has arrived. There is the excitement of having avoided this power they have over you to erase you at will. You break free in the pleasure of finding new grounds, new allies, new columns to lean on. This is what it feels like in the very beginning. So, your time has come, but it's not like you waited for your sisters of the North to fart so you could empty your derrieres. Our faraway sisters have never been of the North anyway and we farted a very long time ago, before the beginning of time. This is the earth-Quake story to tell.

The bird who suddenly realizes they were meant to fly, the grain of sand who finds their soul in others' eyes; a stillness of the sun, of cells, of pores, and bones; we could explode at any moment but the road to pleasure is the struggle itself, and the bliss of doing number two ends at the moment it all comes out. It's nothing like a settlement the moment you wipe yourself out. Here we are mounted by all kinds of pleasures and hungers, dreams and desires, lightheadedness, hope, and invincibility; I can change the world, we can fuck the world, this is what it feels like, in the very beginning.

And the moment comes, you write in the middle of the blank page, I have decided to vomit the garbage they say would save my soul, and sing with Gloria Gaynor, I will survive. You and I have ploughed the land for a very long time, hungry, angry and not knowing what it is we were hungry for; this moment; this is the story to tell the *descendantes*; this split, whole and broken, apart and entangled.

t
The outbreak

You count 93,000. Perhaps you left out one, two, or more.

My skin is of dark roast. At my kitchen table I sit and I pound my fingers to keep up with my heartbeats; can you hear me?

My feet have doubled in size; the hands spread like an open parasol, heavy and snappy; but a cup of coffee is easy to lift; you raise yourself up slowly by pressing your arms on the table; there is also your bottom or, let's say, the heavy feet below the table that slowly give you the ultimate push forward, and here you go with your cup in your mouth. I plug my nose to swallow. I am adding up my days, and it's a bittersweet kind of way to keep breathing.

Perhaps you miss thousands and more.

Perhaps we should start counting together the dead, the fallen, the sick, the many branches, not just one; lots and lots of trees and branches to count leaves on, one by one.

Thousand million of them, one by one and taking a break, a sip, a pause, a sigh after each count. I moan.

A leaf breathes, you know? A leaf hides many other leaves than can ever be seen; many you and I will never count. Should we continue counting?

More than 10,000.

Fallen. Missed.

Counting and continue counting; one by one in the name of the millions we miss; those before 2010; the ones we have never imagined; others we cannot yet see. So many we didn't know about. Those who ploughed the land centuries ago for us to eat.

hmf

Counting and counting is what you do, isn't it; your numbers are proof of your labor; but here you get more digit than can ever be counted, and the real integer is larger than your poll can document. It is that big; more than you can ever repair. Really.

Ask me no more. It is the camouflage Youwès army guard roaming the neighborhood and picking on flies with his lance all day. At night, he would pick up my girls from our house. They were his bonus and happy to be just that. One night he did not come to pick them up; and two mornings after not showing up the youngest of my girls started vomiting; she squeezed all the juice out of her bones. I watched her die and fall at four in the afternoon the day after. The baby in her belly went with her like two rivers joined before they see themselves in two separate basins to meet again later. We don't have a face for the baby. This is what I am telling you: a leaf always hides another. I am aware you have no place in your brain for unseen leaves. Many in the village fell like leaves falling in late September and spreading their seeds to the gods in avalanche. Million didn't make it to the health center in the village or to a proper cemetery; my youngest didn't. For when death takes it on you pitilessly you strike back, you tighten your teeth, roll up your sleeves very high and dig the hole for as much as leaves it can hold, and you throw your heart in it, how can you live after that?

My fallen daughter is underground in my backyard and you're saying you're sorry!? You're talking about apologies!? Making things right!? All the while you say leaves have been falling for a very long time in my backyard!? What kind of apology is that!? I know you don't want to apologize!? You don't give a shit about me counting leaves falling. I know that. But I will continue counting one by one with my hands and with my fingers the fallen, the unseen, the unimagined. Perhaps I'll reach millions, perhaps not. I'll count the hairs over your head, and the pores over your skin, and your sweat I will count one drop after another. I will hunt you each day, each minute, here and everywhere, with my fingers and my heartbeats stomping and counting over a cup of coffee. It takes that much to not sink into your skin.

u
as in Youwès
My friend Marilyn delivered her newborn just last week. She is now planning to return to her workplace. She is a nurse. I am in shock. Shouldn't the nursery business care about the well-being of the newborn? I said to Marilyn I have a friend in another country who just got six months paid parental leave. My friend Marilyn said, yes, the *Youwès* is the only developed country that has not yet passed adequate laws about parental leave. Now I am in shock beyond the magnitude of a Richter scale. It never occurred to me that this is what a developed country looks like. The nurse cannot nurse her own infant but is going to nurse others'.

v
c'est la Vie
I am grateful to be alive now, for the water I drink, and for all the impossible unimaginable dreams. After I am gone, I will not come back. Not in this way. Not in any way. Not now. Not ever. I will not. Twice the *miserere* is unbearable.

w
wave Zero feminism
You see History walking by wearing a big hat like a sombrero over a bony breadstick you don't yet see. But you can tell in the hat's landscape of dust and stars and big countries, as well as their little counterparts that *la raison du plus fort est toujours la meilleure.*

In the southern region of Santo Domingo, female slaves took the streets demanding equal pay for equal work. To silence the slave women, Etienne Polvérel in confidence with his bondmen whisper: "It is not against the owner; it is against yourselves, against their men, that the women formulate these exaggerated pretensions. They do not want any consideration to be given to the inequality of strength that nature has placed between them and the men, to the habitual and periodic infirmities, to the intervals of rest which their pregnancies, their childbirth, their nursing, oblige them to take. These men, whose advantageous portion of the revenues they covet, work, save, and desire money only to be able to lavish it on their women. Africans, if you want to make your women listen to reason, listen to reason yourselves."

You can tell under the large sombrero the lines of that history are crushed inside. For there is first wave, second wave, and third wave. There's even bad wave. But against all that lining up, little history waved things up before History sticks its head out.

xyz
Poeticity

The wounds at the tips of my fingers are as real as the wounds the champions of civilization advocate for. To echo Maryse Condé, I live in a world foreign and empty. I survive with the tools I possess, my x, my y, my z, my shit and their grammar, my alphabet, my wounds, my salvation.

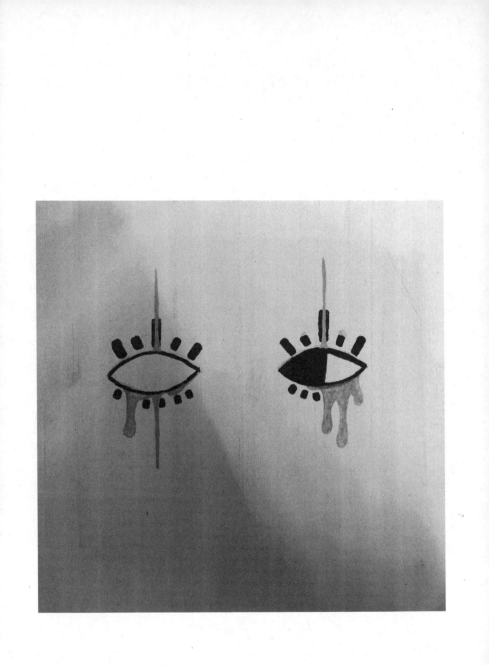

-5-
Nothingness

I.

Every day she gives herself away; piece by piece, one day a spit, another day a morsel of the lung; gradually her water, her cells, or a kidney; and every day nothing comes back.

In ordinary times she opens the door to the quiet dew and squints at the neighborhood shaking off its shadows. She sweeps the wooden floor, opens curtains, rakes leaves, and brings her hoe over her shoulders while her fingers hang on to brushes and feather brooms and pens and paper clips. She is draped in a colored house-apron and a grey pantsuit, all neat. A scarf tames the hair behind her neck. She sometimes catches her breath at her oak kitchen table while sipping coffee and composing days for kids, brothers, husbands, and uncles. The time rolls on.

1804: the year when the ground opened up under the sabots of girls standing like baobabs, girls with no stamps, girls whose legs burst the air.

The developer whispers her name away, and she disavows the moist in her knee pit; she is no longer sure whose body heat shriveled the bedding. She sees the edges of time. She will bear the world and leave no marks. The full moon was not at all poetical, but traces of all times can be felt in the crease of her bones, the sound of nothingness. There's nothing left, except for the lips of Time that lick back and forth on the generosity of her memories. She gives herself away every day, still.

II.

Everyone knows the story of the underground girl who couldn't recall whatever name she pulled under her feet. There was a

Sunday school teacher, the procurer's daughter, the mill owner's daughter, and there was a girl who lived on Calvary Hill. There were girls in no cities. Countless girls there were, across times that can never be redeemed. Girls with no names. So, don't tell me it was a long time ago. Don't tell me about the four waves.

For centuries, the underground girl wouldn't groan her very own name. At her oak kitchen table, she sometimes catches a breath, and to the coffee mug she has nothing to say. She has wondered if it's normal to find nothing to say about stories of decomposition, of girls chasing wind. After a breath that whirls down her spine, she scrapes off the scum on her lips with her teeth. The woman's ground runs parallel to the edge of time in a not at all straight line.

And there was a little boy aboveground who asks the underground if she used to bike when she was little; his sister says, of course.

How do you know? She traded stories for oblivion on a hand-knitted woolen blanket each night. Merry-go-round each night she plays with the girls while running and singing *tifi ki pa konn lave pase chita kay manman w*, their pledge of allegiance. Allegiance she pledges to brothers, fathers, and uncles, her first world. That that is THE WORLD has the taste of unmanageable tales. The boy in her tale holds the bluest eyes and a smile that cups her in his hands, a good omen he says, she says. He laughs. She laughs, now, at her oak kitchen table.

To break the lines, the boy with the brownest eyes sent a letter that begins: I would like to marry your daughter, she is very well ready, and will make me the happiest man of the canton (the richest man, you must read). The forefathers nod, send their daughter off to her destination. This was today; this was some two hundred years ago; but this isn't the way of things. There was only one shack for all the girls and the underground woman has dreamed of a dress of her own. She knew in the moment nothing more than the trap of giving herself away the way the water waves itself away, in countless, endless waves. Now she climbs one mountain after the other, and each cheek of the mountain would always come back and come back different.

III.

At the edge of a rusted cast-iron pot, dusty typewriters typing, remembering, pondering over how to approximate unsettled lines, unseen traces, and times to come.

She's uneasy, not bitter, the underground. She does not rehash her missing years. She does not yell after her offspring or punish them for how they speak their father tongues. Fine. Every once in a while, she rambles about life playing tricks, and she blames the alliances she makes. You go to the street market and do not bring home the first pile of tomatoes you stumble upon. But she does bring home the first pile of tomatoes she stumbles upon, marries, forfeits herself into time made empty, a curse, a trap. On the lines of her palms she runs.

I hear you saying, you know mommy, she for sure used to bike a lot when she was a kid; I say nothing. An oak kitchen table knows the marks of the wind. Nothingness plays tricks, is fallacious for a good cause. I could have done better. My water is oil in emulsion. And I like it there, where the lines are un-seeable.

Underground: womb awaiting, earthquake style, still.

Who does not flinch at the cattle giving away its water under a branding iron? And the lined patterns they make. An old cast-iron coffee pot knows the heartbeat of the land, its palms whose traces were split and rearranged as if to liberate the ground from its secrets. Underground carries hips and secrecies; she fulfills quotas, breeds, and gets whipped; she sleeps on the wooden floors she sweeps; and the times she recalibrates; and the way she gets along. How could you name that, the traces made in the fullness of an emptied moon? She likes it there, or so you say. But the course of her path is to be neither passionate nor disinterested. A cattle's blood and water bear cells, times, desires, and traces and deaths by the millions. Millions more names you miss no matter how well you count. There remains always an afterthought, a storyline, another path, one more name, an ache, un-traced by you.

There was, in the beginning, a plantation. From West to East and from East to the fallacies of the West it's a not at all straight line—I learned to ride in my thirties. When is my name no longer my name?

IV.

With home and family, is how it began. As if there was a point of beginning to begin with.

She shrouded her body under a white dress she bargained for an indemnity. A wedding invitation on a bloodied boiled black sheet of paper, a few merchants with their bouquets, and dead black girls at the last minute will sail a bride against the edge of time. One hole on the left shoulder, one more on the right, the underground is a picture, pinned down. A call to order, no matter how great the restitution, carries the weight of a hammer drill. No more running after imagined realities. The underground could no longer remember how each pin was fixed; sometimes it was like getting a permission before going to a friend's funeral, before arranging the hair in a certain kind of way, sending groceries to the parents, *bay lwa yo manje*, or saying her name. It happened so naturally, she did not give second thoughts to entering the plantation like the foremothers. Isn't evoking the foremothers intriguing? The developer told her he could breed her over and over. Running on the palm of her hands seems much harder. No wonder a bridal is a meanwhile, an in-between. She would erupt in the middle of the night chewing names, lines, and traces she stamped in the spread of her dress. She never left. And yet, you would have to link the world she swerves with the one she is running towards. There are more to the foremothers than how the masters filed them away.

Old smells that stand in the way, belt with no ends, feet walking and sauntering, to the edge of time. Until to the edge of time, the remains of breath waved on old oak kitchen tables.

V.

Dear Wind:

There had been times I thought I could have just covered my nappy strands with dead wigs and not asked the developer to fix the entrance door or sweep or mop. Maybe, I should have let him bring the money home, alone. I wonder when he finally realizes that his name is nothing but a chip, a twist, a vagary, a null. Did he really thought that his epithet was somehow larger than life? Today it rains pox, gonorrhea, credit score, Hollister, and broken glass. It's nothing like a lullaby. But I play hide-and-seek with my ghost and my lover is of thousands of faces. I sail my kite against the howling of the night five times, ten times, and million more. Many more shirts I iron and fold with broken bones. How do you know a ghost is a ghost? I concede the land to my first lover for the bottled plastic water he promises to bring home and the Vibrio Cholerae that comes with it. My ship. My whip. My broken hips. How much longer will you tell me, one is Christian, picks up the first pile of tomatoes at the neighborhood market, consumes, this is love? How many times do I have to tell you nothingness abhors loyalty? My saliva is white as snow. I am the underground with no bows. I roll myself in a carabella wrap dress with no tie, and my paillasse I carry to the top of the Calvary hill house, in the gas station, on the streets, in any streets. The ground, my open boat. When I swirl, it will be another instance, another quake, another geography, another death to birth. The world turns round and round under my skirts. There are names I whisper in my short-legged prayers, then a breath is reduced to dust. But you'll claim rights to ownership, this I know. There's nothing left. I will keep running. The missionaries never left. There must be some kind of logic behind lights and river lines intermingling. I must say goodbye now. To the time that came back and never left, only the ghost is bound to enter and leave the stage.

Earthquake: intent of worlds reshuffling.

VI.

The moment had descended upon her back, a damp cold taking her in. She purses her lips, sips the roasted coffee through her nostrils, sighs, and the memories ripple onwards. In between the walls of darkness, there's a lifetime, a well-constructed hole that gulps, and a scarf eyeing the neck. Whatever happened to burning leaves, their glare, a fleeting glow? There are truths in the hostage room that will not see the day. Regardless, no one is stranger to the black hole.

A rope gradually squeezing the neck
bracing the arms and lacing
the fingers, her legs
that swerve
black hole taking her in
silences that convert torture into a sacred space, a sanctuary
room, a private tour
a hole that is not a passage
Hmf.

Put starch in your laundry; don't walk with your legs open; don't laugh too loud; avoid striding over a broom; keep your Bible under your armpit; smile; your foremothers were very proud and very humble, they knew how to keep their dirty laundry in the dark, hostage room. They can teach you how to patch a world falling in pieces: you snuff yourself out. It was the worst of times. It is the worst of time. Nobody notices anymore that East and West are wicked loopings.

They started coming in the 1400s, by boat, for the gold, the cacaos, the sugarcanes, the cotton, the land. They would keep coming for the right to let live. Sometimes, there was not enough land for the developer; he would go astray, there might be another land, there would be more each time, more water; and more wombs and vaginas, and the right to kill. To cover up his madness, his name became the mark of the gods and the underground was told to have professed chastity and obedience. You fill me up, he says, I will love no one else but you. I will throw myself under the bus one day. It's not your fault nobody ever found gold. *Let's make sure no one knows your name.* Her leaving may happen anytime. He breeds her; others before her have pledged a fate, an allegiance, a common sense, a plea. The gods weeping for redemption. He knows there are lines that she knows that can fill silences like a sponge sucking up water, stories of his haunted self that have their room in the underground. The gods have fallen in disgrace, can you see the waves unleashed? With all the conveniences, the new machines, the GIS, NGS and GPS, the land always returns and returns different. An entrance to nothingness?

VII.

There's nothing left.
Except to face archipelagos arising out of the ripples of winds, and the times they boil in impermanence. The time the Pinta was incorrectly thought to be the first boat. Has anybody noticed: to know is to come across. Now imagine the feel of living on an archipelago like any other and synchronized to all times. 1492 is a trap; 2010, a gauge; 2016, a nuclear apocalypse.

The air was chill at this time of the day as the underground loosens the shawl around her neck, as she stands before winds. Around her neck she unfolds the shawl that she rides and folds and unfolds in the circumvent geographies of cast-iron pots. A rolling ball has no edges, nor a carabella wrap dress. There will be another wind, another town, another people, another language, another lover, another land, and other times to come. How do you start mumbling your name before it's too late?

In the beginning was the Nil.

I hadn't much time. I brought with me all the important papers and a card that says, I love you too. My sisters will keep at their shacks some of my favorite dresses, my old piano book, and a few old photos. I always dream that at any point in time I can return to old songs and to old piano books the way one returns to leftover dust in an empty bedroom. But a shake can crumble, all together, the songs, the old and the new, and the dream of taking a bow and leaving the stage in an endearing dress after playing *Nini et Bébé*. Just *Nini et Bébé*. I didn't go very far. I left for a land of coffee, and my bags still carry a few painted dresses I hadn't worn for a very long time. A dress can tell you so very much about how far you have gone. They are left crumpled and wrinkled, churned and fixated on their own demise. On an oak Saint Paul kitchen table deciding between a bean and a quake, which one is the strongest is a very complex equation. I shall write a postcard to my lover now. Dear RET: I think I am ready for you and me to become an item but I have lost your name to the wind. I am eating banana bread with a café-au-lait in my Murielle Creations dress. I will play guitar with my daughter this summer, oops ... my coffee is too sugary, I am going for a refill. I regret leaving you.

There is the blood she clothes herself with, shroud, atlas, sketches, footprints through which she walks and for which there are no possible algorithms: the clot that patches things over here with things over there, the juice on her sword, the sweat that coats the lands, the spit, the fertilizers, the bellies fed, the breathing going round and around. And the wounds of the potatoes are all vaporous, wraithlike, windlike, un-seeable. And the debt to be paid is everything there is, an underground that is more than an imagined stomping ground. Your Third World, THE WORLD, whose traces on an oak kitchen table will not go away. The print of the underground will travel that far, further than the bluest eyes and will carry the sound of all words and traces.

VIII.

The underground that turns the course of the wind for the freedom she is running after, not the shack she has built but will remember later or the sisters and the mothers she has promised not to leave. The awakening of the people is a no city of names vanished in times made equal, of heaven and earth walking into each other, of devices concocting genes. The gods are dismissed under the principles of procreation. Nothingness is not the backyard, nor the front. You must lay your feet in the dominion to see where one begins and where the other never left. The lesson today was about rivers crossing. It was never in Port-au-Prince, Kingston, or Mexico City—the gods spoke madness. A kangaroo is charged for wanting to return home, a gorilla for going naked, another for shaving their head, and another for having too many pupils. The cow wants to keep their milk. Over the fallacies of times, you would have to tell how the world says your name, how the wind trims your palms; you would have to tell the sound of your knuckles cracking; how you float in faint, in trance, your tornadoes, your times, you would have to tell; it's a court as wide as the sky.

The underground purses the edge of her lips over the oak kitchen table. There remain on the ground a colored house-apron, a shawl, a quake, voices fainting, *tifi ki pa konn lave pase chita kay manman w*, and the ripples of times they open up. One last sip. Another time.

The nothingness, all there is.

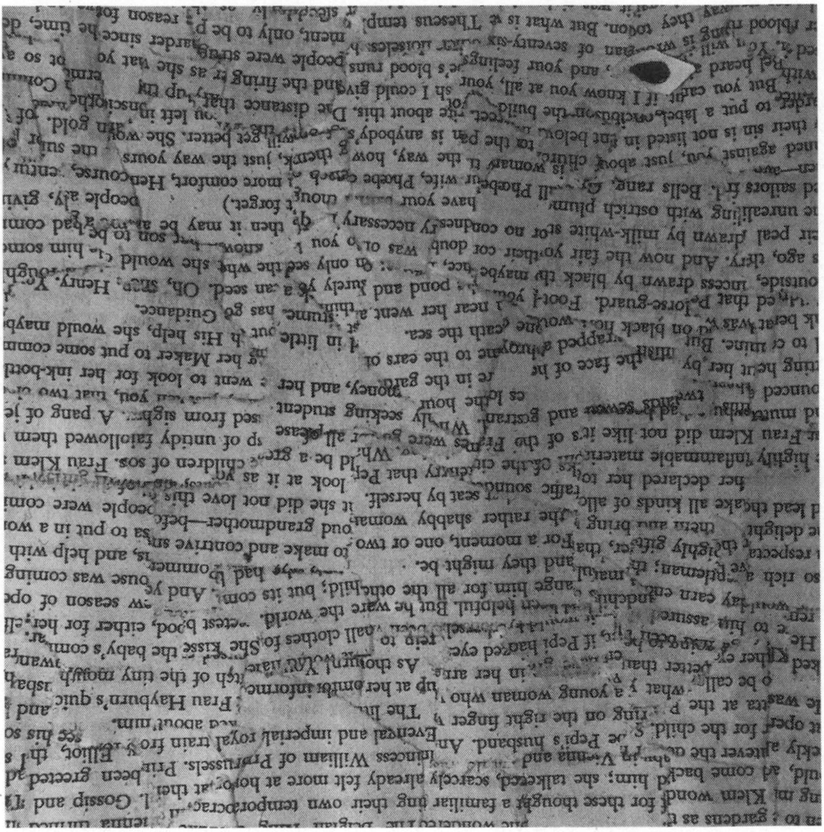

-6-
Hungerlessness

In *Nan Dòmi,* Aunt Tansia tells Mimerose Beaubrun that the body is an inconvenience, not giving a fuss about it is to enter the realm of the gods.

It's Thursday morning, I am on my way to the Keystone food shelf, I have in my purse a copy of *Nan Dòmi,* I will bring home some good food the kids will eat noisily, crunchily, hungrily.

Nan Dòmi, and this is me going on a rant, begins with a prologue, and with Beaubrun and Lòlò fasting. I get rid of the book's preface the same way Beaubrun is learning about her body, the kids and I are not fasting. There is a hunger born out of will-power and another out of convention. The imprisonment of the body like a neighborhood map, is shaped by points of reference.

Time is a queer kind of prison.

I arrive to the Keystone food shelf a few minutes before 10:00 am. You cannot do without food the way you do without time. I wind out of time, it locks me in, and my number is 24. There is, in both time and hunger, the blissfulness of being suspended, and the strengthless neck that puts to rest the feet, the grunting of an angry stomach, and the clocks of a lifetime altogether. With more than two dozen people entangled in the small entrance room of a food shelf station, the breathing between who is who is undecidable, blurred, and foggy. All bodies are made equal in a passage to plenitude.

Aunt Tansia says to Beaubrun, dance my child, dance. In the small entrance room, I am in a trance. I am rereading the second chapter of *Nan Dòmi,* it's a lot like dwelling in a mud volcano and being mounted by a self-fulfillment on the inside, an utter silence on the outside. There's in that bliss a nearness of time, a closeness with hunger of all kinds, a fatal trap to being either a portion of god or a ghost of yourself. Stillness is times made equal.

I am going to kick ass this summer.

Yesterday my daughter opens the refrigerator's door and there she goes, *doooh, there's nothing to eat today*. Taking hunger for granted is to silence the body. The smell of a small entrance room will give you the illusion of people rolling on the same clock and swimming in the same hunger. When I say the 'a' word my daughter blows up like a scandalous stuffy nose holding together in rage both the stuff of the nose and the promise of its imminent eruption. So, when I tell you I am going to kick butts, I truly am. Within a superposition of times and hungers, I am at the Keystone station for at least one hour, to stay still. With *Nan Dòmi*. In a small food shelf entrance room.

In the stillness of the Keystone's entrance room, I am eye to eye, nose to nose, but not shoulders to shoulders with a tall black fellow.

The bonding principle is stranger to the gaze. In the gazing one assumes they know the kind of body the other holds. The tall black guy gazes at me every minute or so. I am dwelling in *Nan Dòmi*. Beaubrun is telling about the dreamer, and my eyes are popping out, and each line of the chapter is a punch to my chest. I am craving for more. *There Is No Body To Know* will be the title of my presentation for the feminist studies conference this year. One must get completely naked, Aunt Ansia advises. The tall black guy has very long legs. He is throwing his eyeballs at me and I am like, bring it on, baby. I am used to the gaze. *Nan Dòmi* begins with a preface that will tell you all there is to know about some-body. But any-body has other ways to get around. I am reading and I am all sweaty and shuffled. I am sinking. A prologue and not a preface will hold the gaze of a tall black guy. Holy shhhhhugar! Karen Barad writing about quantum entanglement and diffraction has nothing on Aunt Tansia speaking through Beaubrun.

Time is the woman chewing hungrily she will not fuck with someone who clothes their plate at a Keystone food shelf station.

I lean my back against the wall of the small entrance room. The question is, why does Aunt Tansia choose to go without food. The English version of *Nan Dòmi* lies in a light blue cover and I fucking love it—oops the f-woooord. A hiatus is a lively tension, not a gap, this one again is for my daughter who doesn't like it when I say shit. I glance at the tall black guy who wears gray sweatpants and a t-shirt of the same color. A time curls onto another through loops and skips and splashes in upsetting ways; the-ways-we-know that time expunges; and you have a loop and a skip splashing away others. The way we gaze as if time stood still. There is no such thing as the stillness of time. There is selectiveness, there is the Time, and there are Times in différance. Aunt Tansia advises Beaubrun to let her body manage itself. I will let my eyes wink, wander, just a little to begin with.

The smartest guy I have ever dated would sometimes pick up his bread at a community food shelf. With him holding several doctorates, steady geography lines, plus his own topography, I had to let him go, and there are three kinds of hunger. There is the man who speaks too muchly too loud even when he's not speaking. There is the drummer who taps the drum; a drummer thinks his waves and turbulences are all there is. Maybe the tall black guy has loose geography lines which, in the eyes of the hungry woman, would save him from sitting in a plagued food shelf entrance room.

Now is the moment to let the eyes wander, to gaze, I am going to let you know I know you're staring at me. But staring at people when you meet them eye to eye and nose to nose, but not shoulders to shoulders is a fudging embarrassing embarrassment. I give up. I pull out from my purse Hugh Prather's *Notes to Myself*, and what happens is just that: when you put together Prather and Barad and Beaubrun, the tension escalates. Without knowing you fuck yourself, the books, and everyone else in between, including a tall black guy who wears gray sweatpants and a t-shirt of the same color! My daughter doesn't like the f-word either and I don't give a fudge about what my daughter wants. Another hunger has the like of Aunt Tansia for whom emptiness is road to pleasureness and to uneasiness. In the small entrance room of the Keystone food shelf station, there is a closeness to breathing at zero degrees Fahrenheit, a nearness to death, a silencing of all cares. There is the body reduced to a glass of water, a bliss, a vacuum, a non-retour.

***

—Number 24!

I am a number. I stand up. I smile light at the tall black guy who wears gray sweatpants and a t-shirt of the same color. I wink. That will be all I'll do to you. More than that is resetting the clock back to zero. Don't get me wrong, I love Karen Barad but it doesn't cost to flirt a little. Don't cling to anything my girl, you are a dreamer, Aunt Tansia warns Beaubrun. The road of emptiness is that of all senses, of complete insensibility. Aunt Tansia without an elementary school diploma doing quantum entanglement is a disjuncture to time.

I do Keystone on Thursdays mornings, once or twice a month when the food shelf carries fresh produce. I say hello to Debbie who registers everyone who comes in. I give her my ticket. My name at least for now is 24. I once asked Debbie about her name and Debbie smiled at me and Debbie said to me my name is Debbie. Debbie has a double chin and a generous smile. Her eyes that confess I am happy to see you are the clock jumping backward a few minutes to midnight. Debbie knows a thing or two about how much money she saves me with every food shelf visit. She will never know how much a cart fully foodly loaded will change the past. I talk about how beautiful the weather is to not talk about things she does not need to know. I will ask Annie and Max to make a beautiful artful thankful card for beautiful Debbie. I am also due to write our American story hunting for food.

A food shelf will put on your table foods you do not see at the store. Organic fresh fruits and vegetables that have become a kind of unwanted entanglement after they have reached the pantry of some bodies, the moment time expires on the less than humans. You've been flirting with the vacuum all along, until comes the bliss that blows all of your selves away and puts you in pieces; not because for the next two weeks unwanted fresh fruits and vegetables will not be a problem, but for being wrapped up by a kind of hunger you did not know you were hungry for.

As a kid, I was a member of a children's choir; we flirted with times in our bones when singing *En son temps*.

I would go without food the day of a singing performance, for the bliss of contemplating a breaking apart of my body, a conjuring of selves not yet known, a pleasure I pursued later on during my years in collegiality with dead white men. My flesh now and then dwells on itself with a strong feeling of contempt, a fierce protest against the betrayal of a certain kind of caring. Here, my hunger becomes the experience and the road to things that reside in silence; an enlightenment; an antidote to the imprisonment of thought, to the negation of beingness. No center, no point of reference to pleasuring, no geography lines to feeding, to knowing, to writing, and to everything else.

I am still at the food shelf, indulge me. I proceed after checking with Debbie. Another staff member of the food shelf, who is not the tall black guy wearing gray sweatpants and a t-shirt of the same color, will write my name on a piece of paper while telling me he will try to sound my name right. No surprise here. Number 24 is dead! I will try to read your name, he says, and see if I get it right. I indulge him. This is how he says hello each time I visit. With his beautiful smile, a nice barb cut, and thin lips, you do not care whether the white man barks or whispers. I ask him for his name. I tell him Al is beautiful. No, he speaks back and he shakes his head, your name is beautiful. I insist. Al is beautiful and sweet! I win. I push the cart before me. The eyes of the tall black guy wearing gray sweatpants and a t-shirt of the same color weighs heavily on my back. A tall black guy wearing gray sweatpants and a t-shirt of the same color eyeing my underpants, and not Al, troubles me a great deal. But how do I know? I don't. I am in shutdown mode. The lines on my forehead are still and my lips are sealed and my legs stay locked. A man who carries a nose with the width of an umbrella is not to be trusted, they say.

And I am in the Keystone food shelf this Thursday morning because I enjoy watching my 6-year-old son eating with good appetite, angrily, hungrily, happily. He, too, carries a nose with the width of an umbrella. As he grows older, I am hoping he will refrain from filling up his body with the bondage of three meals a day, which would take over other hungers, put them to rest. In *Nan Dòmi*, these hungers uncover layers of consciousness. It's a shifting ground to get rid of the body's bond of attachments. Aunt Tansia says so.

Three quarts of a gallon 1% milk, one of them will sit in the freezer; jicama sticks from Cub Foods I have yet to try, they-rarely-go-on-sale; thanks-a-lot Girl Scout cookies; organic edamame soy beans in shells; green beans in almond butter sauce; mango salsa, cauliflower rice, and Siggi's-simple-ingredients-not-a-lot-of-sugar yogurts; Tazo chai decaf tea, dried cranberries packs; holy shhhhhugar, chocolate bars; I-am-going-to-indulge-myself-in-lots-of-writings-this-afternoon-while-drinking-tea and-choco-late; baking mix pancake flour, organic popcorn, organic tortilla chips, angus beef hotdogs, a large family pizza, we-are-here-for-a-great-Friday-movie-night-tomorrow; chips, guacamole, oranges, and fresh apples; three avocados in a bag, pita breads, small ba-gels; the-kids-are-going-to-be-so happy; Jesus! Annie's Macaroni and cheese and cookies; one-gallon-of-apple-juice-is-enough; rice, beans, spaghetti, etcetera; etcetera; etcetera. Senses shuttered for other voyages, no matter the cost of staying with the body a little longer, in wait of being enlightened, one more time.

In a logical disjunction Beaubrun writes about her partner, Lòlò, accompanying her in *Nan Dòmi*.

I ponder over the kind of company one goes to bed with, whether this company is the partner, the community, the disease by which the flesh abides, the food that feeds the stomach, de-ranges it or the knowledge that shapes a war's battles and twists the rolling of times in history books. Lòlò is present throughout the narrative in his own way, not overtly; he is not an absence, nor a background. He is a layer of consciousness in Beaubrun's *Nan Dòmi*, of Beaubrun journeying in her state of sleeping; he is a portion of his own self, of Beaubrun too. Aunt Tansia advises, avert your gaze every time you feel attracted by something in order to gain the mastery of the *je*. One must say no to company that oppresses, swallows, and takes over. I must travel with those seized by the same hunger, with almost the same anger, with irre-solvable internal hunger. I must be daring enough to walk alone, the way Beaubrun journeys in *Nan Dòmi* and grants her body the anger to linger in hunger.

Some years ago, I had a fibroid the size of a six months old fe-tus removed from my flesh, from my body, my selves. After the sur-gery, I asked the surgeon to bring me the fibroid so I can sit with it, dialog with it, and graze with. I wanted to introduce myself to it in a way we have not been before. My fibroid was a co-traveler, not an inconvenience to get rid of and toss away anyway anyhow. So now you are mumbling, who are your co-travelers?

The gaze of the tall black guy wearing gray sweatpants and a t-shirt of the same color descends upon my back in a kind of symmetrical way, his right hand holds onto an Aldi plastic bag. I have now in my cart enough junks and groceries to make the kids happy for the entire week, and I have only two in case you are wondering. My Dad and my Mom had six of us when they were stranded in Port-au-Prince. My parents in a food shelf station some twenty years ago would have been like finding repose in the desert of exile. Me, walking towards the scale to weigh my food is like carrying forth the flavor of fresh rotten candies and disjointed times with no expiration date. This is it. None of us should have expiration dates. *Nothing Ever Dies* by Viet Thanh Nguyen is the title of the book I will start reading next month. It is quite an irony that I visit the Keystone food shelf twice a month to feed my family's hunger in the land of Uncle Sam. My dad in exile in his own country, after Tonton Sam took matters in hands and overthrew, even in the asymmetry of things, had no such a thing.

***

The body remains boundless in both the physical and the spiritual, Aunt Tansia explains to Beaubrun. Hungerlessness could be indeed, hmf, a quest for dwelling within times, senses, and bodies outside of measurements. But this Thursday morning, I carry a number, a weight, an expiration date.

As a means of getting through I will weigh my food before leaving the food shelf station. I do not remove the fruits and vegetables from the cart as the staff often urges us to. Water drops from the lettuce bring to my nostrils the murmurs of faraway Sunday mornings deprived of greens. I'm thirsty now.

A beautiful lady with a pretty face who assists shoppers with the scale, helps me transfer fruits, vegetables, and breads to another cart; they do not get weighed. I will help you, I say, and I remove from before my nose fruits and vegetables and crunchy-brown-garlic-honey-coated breads. It's a lot like trading fingerprints with the *boulangers*. I am careful not to open my armpits too wide; I am sweaty. My morning shirt did not come fresh from the laundry machine. The lady helper has sweet biometrics and a name, Mickayla, fresh like morning dews on *choublack*.

I have not seen Mickayla in a while. She was not here during my last food shelf visit, although I saw her at Aldi a few weeks ago. Mickayla doesn't know that I saw her at Aldi. I did not say hello but sneak-peeked at her in between Aldi's aisles. I told Mickayla I missed seeing her. It's true. The food at Aldi is less expensive than at Cub's. This is why I shop at Aldi. The tall black guy wearing gray sweatpants and a t-shirt with the same color with an Aldi plastic bag in his right hand probably knows a thing or two about Aldi's cheap organic fruits and vegetables, and per-haps, about me.

I walk towards the end of the room where I will pack my food. There, I pick up additional items, tomatoes, fresh lemons from the farm, and a pair of *mirlitons* I will not cook. How do you say that in English? Chayotte. Disgusting! The kids and I drink lem-on water every morning before heading out to school or to work or to whatever else. Sometimes we mix the lemon with a piece of dark chocolate into our guts. Each day, you hope that in the first hour of the day you will prepare your body for anything to come. But again, words are just that, words, words, worlds. The body of a Chayotte has its own way of getting around, ways reason itself does not know, Aunt Tansia says so, to Beaubrun.

There are three possible ways I mutter the word food. First, my dad repeats all the time that a real man quits his bed in the morning before anyone else in the household. So, Dad regularly wakes up at the dawn of the day, blends his breadfruit, brews his coffee, and cuts through the day. Second, food is religion where it is rare and getting food on the table is its own rituals. Today I place a spaghetti squash in my fully loaded food cart, and 10 minutes is all I need to pack, arrange everything, leave the food shelf for good, and un-ritualize myself. And to proceed with a liturgy of another sort, I will call Mom in the afternoon, ask her about what she ate in the morning, I am softening my guilt of having too much. I also think of food in the way of plastic, chem-icals, oils, stocks, and western fictions stuffed into one's stom-ach and brain, and which turn the body with its own knowledge, memory, and spirituality into waste and garbage cans. It seems to me that for each body buried under junk and chemicals and the dead white man, there is a civilization that goes wasted.

The tall black guy wearing gray sweatpants and a t-shirt of the same color with an Aldi plastic bag in his right hand stands right behind me. He has very little amount of food in his cart.

He probably has a small family. Maybe the food is just for himself. Perhaps, he dwells in hungerlessness. I smile at him. I mutter just loud enough to hear myself mumbling and not speaking, I am almost done, I will get out of your way asap. Beside my eyes, maybe he likes my accent.

Like when I drove to the gas station two days ago for five dollars gas, and the teller chased me outside to hand me a discount coupon. Excuse me, he said at the same time, where are you from? I mean, I love your accent. I am from Haiti. And in my head, I am going with an exasperated what the fuck, Haiti not Paris, disappointed? I asked him right back, where is your accent come from, and I saw him dangling on his two feet, I added very quickly as he was raising his eyebrows, I mean you, and your ancestors too. Then I left. I went right back to my car not caring for his answer which I don't need to hear anyway. I bet he is still figuring out what kind of question was that or maybe he shouted at my car muffling and roaring, is this woman crazy, doesn't she realize I have no accent, with his gas coupon between his fingers and planted on his two American feet in the middle of the gas station.

The tall black guy wearing gray sweatpants and a t-shirt of the same color and with an Aldi plastic bag in his right hand hears me sigh. He gazes at me for a good ten seconds. I am so far away from this moment, so close. There is another way in which I mutter the word food, and it is to remain in a state of hungerlessness. I am an angry back woman.

Now I am seeking a way out.

Everything is going atomic clock, global time, universal time, cosmic time, Barad tells in her video talk, *Undoing the Future*. She ponders over the manner we are synchronized and tied to a particular universal time. The body at any stages at any times never leaves any stage nor any time. With its memory, knowledge, and plagues, and its ways of getting around, the body recalibrates itself toward all moments, paths, senses, times, and knowledge. And towards other bodies, like in Mimerose and Aunt Tansia.

Beaubrun sharing with her readers the philosophy, knowledge, and wisdom, she says, she literally collected from Aunt Tansia, an elderly woman living in rural Haiti who did not make it to school is what I call putting the world back on its axis. Besides, don't go and think that there is a neat separation between Beaubrun and Aunt Tansia, or that the two women and their bodies are determinately propertied. The whole *Nan Dòmi* thing is Beaubrun's own knowledge. *Nan Dòmi* is the teaching and the knowledge of Aunt Tansia. With its light blue cover, *Nan Dòmi* sits in my purse in a keystone food shelf station.

I must go home now.

I will leave my cart near the entrance door to make it easier to bring the food outside, I share with Debbie. Debbie smiles, yes, of course. On the sidewalk, I proceed towards my car, my shoulders are straight, I have given up on hiding how very hungry I am behind a large pair of sunglasses. Now, every passerby can see in my eyes how very well hungry and fucked up I am. I don't know anyhow anymore how to talk out my oppression; how to carry it with pride. I don't know how to deal with being an oppressor myself. I voyage in my state of hunger with both eyes open, with my shoulders straight, that's all. The food in my cart? I worked for it, if you ask me. My country paid for it too, when giving away their *diri latibonit*, their *poul kreyòl*, and *kochon kreyòl* and the land altogether. When giving asylum papers to Miami Rice and beans. I am very well fucked up, angry, and hungry as hell, for air, for food, for some kind of mention that will give me my moment in this time, in no time. I dwell in this hunger, my every day voyage, that I carry some Thursdays behind a cart fully foodly loaded, the kind of moment my dad and my mom never had.

I am spitting out all these things, and pushing the cart before me, and leaving behind the troubled small food shelf entrance room. I am angry. To ease my anger and the guilt of having too much to eat, I will borrow some money, and make a money transfer to my family. But there is no way to ease the guilt of knowing that in exile in his own country, my father sold one by one his pans, his lands, his buckets, and his cars to feed us all after being thrown away by Tonton Sam.

Here I am, carrying one of the groceries boxes to the car. The tall black guy wearing gray sweatpants and a t-shirt of the same color and with an Aldi plastic bag in his right hand who heard me sigh asks me with a very gentle voice if I need help. I choked, I am hesitant, confused; he makes up his mind, Okay you're fine. Okay I am fine, and the second right after he holds me the door, takes the groceries box from my hands that he carries near the car. In truth, what I should be hungry for is to make less pronouncements.

I continue with my rumination, ask myself whether or not he has a ride. And he goes right back inside the entrance room to lift the larger box from my cart, and I open the car's trunk, and he drops off the box inside. I still do not ask him whether he has a ride, I am happy the trunk of my car is clean, a rare instance. I ask him for his name; I ask him to spell it; I say to him his name is beautiful; he says with a louder voice with his head nodding up and down, next time we will talk; I said yes that would be great; he said, really? I said yes. He asks me for my phone number, I will see you again for sure; maybe next month? I had many excuses to not ask him if he needs a ride, among them, the fact that he may not have one, and in that case, I would have to give him a ride with the risk of riding with a serial killer. This is the kind of garbage you are fed with when you eat and learn and watch junk and chemicals three times a day or more.

The minute after he spells it, I have forgotten the name of the tall black guy wearing gray sweatpants and a t-shirt with the same color and with an Aldi plastic bag in his right hand who heard me sigh and carried to my car my boxes full of groceries.

I arrive home, grab a pair of scissors, rip off the introduction chapter of *Nan Dòmi*. Can we speak the truth from the confinement of a center? The body holds the memories and the traces of all times. Thank you Beaubrun for sharing Aunt Tansia with me. The knowledge and the philosophies of the Aunt Tansia I have come to know through you begins with your prologue, with your knowledge, with your worlds, your words, not with an introduction synchronized and trapped to a time made universal. My body is not selectiveness, this time.

Now, in all fairness, the thing for you to do, reader, is to tell me to go fuck off. A tall black guy wearing gray sweatpants, and a t-shirt of the same color, and with an Aldi plastic bag in his right hand who heard me sigh, and helped me with my grocery cart, and asks me for my name with a gentle voice is just like any one of us who happens to pick their bread at the food shelf or at the nearest Aldi, not because they are of a lesser body, of a lesser time, of a lesser name. This is the ways of things. It is just that.

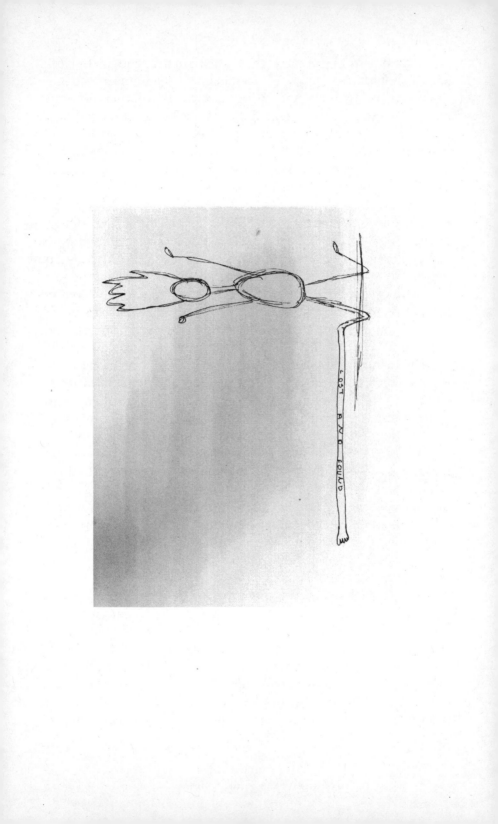

-7-
I Want a Trial

The loaf of bread

I will not leave
hmph
I won't be bound
that is one fucking piece of bread we have here;
The rain spits on all of us don't you think?
do you know how much this bread weighs, witness her gown;
How would I know? They cannot just show up and dispose of me like the loaf of bread you're holding; I am no piece of bread, God knows; where did you get that bread anyway?
rain beads carry intention, they know the binary of things, you know;
I don't, but they do; they know me; they say they know my whereabouts, my becoming, my being me; they say their home is their own; I knew of the empty fire but now need self-flagellation before I can go on and say they don't know me; what if I drift? You want to rid yourself of how they think they know you, but you ramble and you rumble; I cannot even drift for a minute;
how so?
One kicks on one side, another kicks on another side of me, and they stitch and they chip and they fiddle. One makes a pass over here; another transitions the pass to somewhere beyond their visibility; it's a good thing they can't see beyond the tip of their nose, but many more passings here and there I get. They fasten, they stretch, and stiffen at each pass. As for me I roll and dangle in between their feet and on every ground like pitter pattering beads kicking and swaying away; I am the rolling ball who always returns at their feet, but who returns on a different side; I give them equilibrium, that's it.
i like that word;
Me too.

equilibrium, hum, it's like the name of a Whollywood movie;
Really?
    wholly really, the fire burning smaller;
You're about to leave the store and waiting for your change from the cashier. No, I am not from Kenya, yes, I have an accent, then, how is your government, and they let you know they applaud you to have escaped the worst. The moment stinks, it feels like a punishment, and you want to run as fast as you can. They have culture; they know a thing or two about things happening on every ground. So, they already know all there is to know about how the Kenyan government is doing. And you're saying to yourself, I am not the well-behaved child they think I am, so perhaps they should get a glimpse of the sound of memory and you're ready to give up your change in exchange of an hour of history lessons. Then the enormous effort you make to be a good kid and not ask them about banter talks and grabbing moves and genocides and hunger in their house. To stay in between you play the dummy who is always stunned and confounded, what about the government, did something happen, I know nothing, can you tell me?
    the sound memory makes;
Then, they take a step back, they no longer know what to say, and they mumble and hint, earthquake? corruption? Doubalier? or how they've heard about something, anything or anyone that happened years ago, many years ago, centuries ago, ages ago or whatever pops in their mind; and they're looking at you, they want a pass, and you're soo suddenly too serious and too much interested; that you always fail to give them a pass is the worst.
    and then?
I say nothing;
    you say nothing;
I relax, I pose, I breathe. I look at them straight in the eye. This is good and free entertainment, so I am enjoying myself. I wait, you know, for them to formulate something, an idea or to finish their thought, their sentences. It's like me saying you don't know what you're talking about, children. Remember, I'm always the ball that returns at their feet, and always return on myself on a different side.
    really?
Really wholly really. Then they glimpse at my arms fallen down

my body and realize they can't count on me to stuff up their memory brains; I am not even qualified to finish their sentences. My eyes are reddish and worn and half open, which means I don't applaud their applause. It's much worse here. So, I am like, man, I don't know what you're talking about. Their fire getting smaller, you know, and wanting to make a history out of a nothing, see what I mean? And I swear, some obscure part of me just wants to drop my grocery bags right at their station to fill in their guts and give them a run for their money.

and your words do not truly fall out of your mouth, am I right?

No, no, no, my man, it's all happening right here, the inner eye, the inner memory, from the ear to my gut and to my feet and to the ground, the home that is not my own, what can I say? Imagine you're walking your way, and just like the rain beads we were talking about earlier, you see them running towards you, you already sense what's coming, you're joyful and you're not and you're numb, and they hit the bulk of your head with intention and in fury to remind you you're getting a little bit too comfortable here, you shouldn't, even if they say you shall assimilate and speak their language. There's no inner tremor their own memory would make.

ouchchchch

That hurts, I am telling you. So, I am like, how about the shits in your own government? Of course, they do no shit, they have no shits, they are no shits, their shit they don't have carries no sense of being, no sense of memory, no traces of culture, not even the void of the open air. But you know, they are busy playing ball with me at their feet; and home is not where the wind blows; see what I mean?

yikes

Besides, I give them purpose.

how?

You know

i don't;

Well ... the self-assessed standardized human not fully awakened in the late morning dew will want to catch the sound memory makes; they go on with the day deeply swimming and fully asleep in a how-great-thou-heart sea vision; they move on beautifully and dutifully; they run one shift after another and one deed after the next; at the end of the day, they arrive home at night wanting to catch the sound of memory but can't; their cavities are clogged, stuffed up with Burger Kings, deed, shift, and Dr. Phil episodes which keep them fully busy and fully awake days and nights with their eyes wide open on the prize, on any prize they sought, they don't know yet the prize they're running after so it's best to keep going; and the next morning and each morning they continue to give away blood, vessels, sweat, and genes and abilities for God knows what, for prizes they sought; from time to time some lift their heads from the rolling ball I am, just a little, then get back to rolling and kicking again.

and then?

Well ... you know, no one goes home for god sake; their shit is not shitty enough, does not smell bad enough; and suddenly a voice is calling them.

what happens then?

They tweak the storyline, this is what they always do, you know, I am always the problem no matter how shitty their shit is. And the human supposedly standard and standardized has suddenly increased in value; it's like God has revealed himself.

how so? I am impatient my man ... don't make me suffer;

Well ... we remain the one that needs a savior; and they go on missioning, on planting flags; on bringing democracy and en-lightened thoughts; they go giving Jesus away for some bright green bills in their pockets.

I think I am getting it ...

Great, here's how it works. The day comes when you're alone and lonely and shitty and forced to face your shit; you come to real-ize how deeply stuffed up you are with ghosts of Ben Franklins, of lurid dreams, and unreached points clogging your hearts, your vessels, your tissues, your visions; you are a ghost of yourself; and you realize you are tired of running from one debt collector to another; from the mortgage and from the health doctor to pay no matter what to having no time, no rest, no sleep, no body. The day comes where the old vision is suddenly replaced by another one coming from God, brighter than the ghost dream and strong enough to pass for godly revelations and gather followers;

so you are saying missionary workers and democracy artisans and all the other laborers are drowning you fully dull, fully asleep, fully happy?

Yes. You get it, man. It's a kind of consciousness, a moral value you can own, to learn to profess to go save the wretched of the earth and fully knowing that those you pretend to save are the ones saving you. Can't you see how the standard human supposedly standardized is always running to retiring or living somewhere else no matter how bad they profess things over there are? And they get over there where things are supposedly not human enough as developers or artisans or missionaries to get the kind of life they never had on stolen land, free of debt, better schools for their children and they will no longer run all day to unearth the money for their mortgage or taking pill after pill to sleep a little at night with their brain shrinking to the size of a gray quarter. The dream has finally come true for the savior bringing salvation to the wretched and the sinner. This symmetry that keeps on repeating itself, it's not fair.

i see, i see. You're freaking me out man …

In the meantime, I take away their job, their food, their dreams. And I should be grateful when not yet deported; and when not yet deported, I am to teach them a thing or two about world culture. So, I, too, ask them where the fuck they come from? From which country they or their parents immigrated; well … unless you are an Ojibwe, no, honey—you are not that obvious to me; please give the history lessons I need.

hahhaha, you are funny as hell.

I know, I know. You know, I like talking with you.

i do too, you always give me a good laugh, man;

Do you know how to bake a delicious loaf of bread, by the way? I know you're thinking anything bread is fine; but not all breads are breads;

well this looks a very fine bread to me; how about we take care of it right now? there are breads that cannot wait and this, sure, looks delicious;

no kidding, no kidding,

i mean the bread you eat in the afternoon with your tea instead of the biscotti; that makes you think of lemon but has no lemon in it; sweet but without sugar and you don't even need to warm it up or toast it; that kind of bread, I mean. I may need to warm

up this one though; wait a minute, wait a minute.
You know a jungle stays a jungle, you come and cut your way through the bushes, displace the trees, build railroads and you think you now possess the jungle?
do I? holy moly really.
I mean not you, you, you got me man; I mean just because someone shows up and make the laws doesn't mean they have the primacy of law.
pri- pri-macey; is that correct? It's a very fine word here.
Pri-ma-cy, you open your mouth very big on the first syllable, and you show your teeth very very large, like that, PRI-ma-cy, you open your inner body hole on the second syllable. The landing on the last syllable must be soft and gentle.
PRI-ma-cey;
Yes, you get it, it means, they cannot just clap their fingers and think I will not stomp my feet, I don't know if you get me. I know the sound memory makes, don't I?
okay, it's like me who has never imagined a bread talking? Now I am listening to you and I am thinking that a slice of bread may very well talk. Don't you think?
You're correct; the bread has its own law and memory;
what do you think the bread would say?
How the hell should I know, I am not a piece of bread.
but we want to know the language of the bread;
Let me get this straight for you; I don't want to know it; I want them to know mine;
but the bread may want you to know theirs.
I see, you are saying something very important here …
you know, sometimes I think big too.
I will make an appeal;
will you?
I will ask them to present their case;
and what will you say for your case?
I don't know, should I? What can I say? that tonton sam has stripped away our lands and all of our resources, well … tonton sam is a grabber anywhere anytime everywhere, don't you think?
you're correct, man
Maybe, I should tell them about the pig slaughter? Or the Miami

rice invasion? Maybe I should chip them some memory?
maybe, maybe
Really?
really holy moly.
Hell no! I mean, of course, it's all of those things too. But …
what?
You know what? I will only say this, this is my jungle; there's nothing they can do about it; they should get a life!
they should get a life;
Fuck'em!
fuck'em
Fuck me
fuck you
It's a one-pound loaf of bread, plus the weight of a handful of beans, don't you think?
beans carry intentions
I don't want to leave.

Holes

She said she was born this year or that year; as if she came to repair a tissue of holes; like upon her arrival she patches things up and the world is round again. What I see is a bunch of holes; holes that blink; holes that grow; holes that repeat themselves and pop out of one another, one after the other; unruly holes I see.

So, you're saying we persist too hard? We should not get used to ourselves? I say, yesterday has not prepared us for what's coming. We are, each time, holes within holes, a discharge, a disappearance, a do-over. I sometimes manufacture holes to escape, see what I mean?

The cloth that covers the table is covered with holes. We turned it upside down the other day to hide brown spots of chocolate, of grease and black beans, and we pulled one side of the table cloth all the way down to hide a big fat hole. For a moment, you think an open hole is vanished, and your guests will show up and find a clean dining room. But you turn yourself around the table corner and what you see is yourself growing smaller in each hole, in each spot.

We make holes, stains, and torn fabrics go away, turn them over and upside down, drag the edge in the middle, then fold the tablecloth in half until the parts are all used up and exposed and here we are, all churned up and just good for the laundry basket. We are becoming anew. This is the way of things to have wholes out of separate holes.

Our sofa grows holes, too. Our living room floor is always dirty with stuffing furling up from the bottom of the sofa. We pick them up with a broom every hour of every day. I never get tired of cleaning up the mess holes make. It never occurred to me to repair the holes in our sofa. And I have given up the habits of sewing the holes in my skirts and in my green leather jacket or repairing the carpet's depression or the cracks in the window screens or how slow I am. Not all holes need patching up.

And each day I gaze through the window at the open holes in the oak trees and listen to Passenger singing "there's a hole in my bucket" to start counting the thousands of billions of holes of distance between my parents and me. There are holes in your cheekbones. That is also the ways of us; that is also the ways of things.

A wilderness of holes we are: the bushes and the cracks and the puddles and the desires within the pit of your stomach; and our stomachs and our angers, our big fat holes. Now what you see of me is a whole, a making sense, a direction. What I hope you could see is a bunch of holes, unruly uncontrollable wholly holes that don't need cover up.

Grocery Shopping

I am going grocery shopping   at Aldi
it's Wednesday today and almost the end of the month and
      some months it's a Thursday or a Friday   I go to the
Aldi on University Ave
pick up the organic banana the carrots the bacon and the buttered croissants
          I can't afford at Target at Cub at Walmart
I will also bring home from Aldi a $3.40 small yellow bag of coffee Bustelo then
drive a few blocks   down to the Sun Food store
pick up yucca plantains smoked herrings and some fresh potatoes   there is
a shower curtain and cotton swabs andband aids to bring home

                    I will then drive backwards on University Ave
to the Midway Dollar Store logged in the middle of a Cub and a Target
                    that demand $3 in exchange of a sweet potato root
I shop by accident   once in a while at Cub or at Target or at Walmart neighboring
Aldi on University Ave to
     pay $3 for a rotten sweet potato
that never goes on sale
          Aldi is an arbitration ground you pay the carrots the bacon and the sweet potato root for a price within your means
               there's no reason not to dispute the ethic of a $3 cloned sweet potato   And after all the driving upward backwards on University Avenue
theres a goodwill in the same block to which I will run
to space my breath
          Early in the morning I drop the kids at their bus stop
          and
early before that   at precisely 8:40 the same morning
          I open the apartment s door yell   getout now you re
late   I will not drop you off at school I am serious   VLAN
                              I am going
to work in a half hour   being late is a thing
someone   you don't know who exactly
   you know exactly   who keeps you in check
          all of you   Every morning of every day and throughout the day the kids and I race run crosscut and shop   its very possible to sit early morning in the yellow bus not yet at the bus stop and see yourself tied to a $3 small sweet potato root that will leave Aldi s shelves later in the afternoon   in exchange for 60 cents
I just assumed that driving back and forth and standing while sitting and running while sleeping was part of the process of things you do all day and get used to
     not something to fuss about   h u m a n -
nessstandardizedandnormalized

        I teach for a living
my syllabus reads   students
may bring their kids   in the classroom if they have an
emergency   a carte blanche for me
        too   although max and annie in my gender
and global politics course is unthinkably unimaginable
        once or twice every quarter of the year they will miss the
bus   a backup plan is something you put in place
carefully when running all day and dropping yourself every
hour at a grocery store is what you do
Ooh shoooottt
        the bus had just left
        the bus driver could have waited just a little more
instead we are left on the sidewalk standing   in dismay
                        but not for long
        and we rush back to the apartment
I am pissed   I do not have the composure nor the time to
catch the kids feelings nor do I want to have the time to catch
the kidz feelings   nor I want the composure to catch the
kids' feelings
        I take the lead of the three of us taking the stairs back
home   I am angry and I say to them and my tone is
harsh and dry and I do not look at them in the eyes
        you're going to sit properly in the living room for I need to
run teach at the university right now right now this is how I pay
the rent and feed you a $3 unwanted cloned sweet potato I will
be back in two hours to drop you off at school
                        and I do the whole thing   as
if missing the bus is all their fault
        I just assumed that running is what one does and driving a
half hour to save a few cents is the normalcy of things of the everyday   that even with running all day back and
forth and sleeping in a carrel with no windows no room to
breathe one could not afford to be late or wet your bed or chew
on your t-shirt collar or carry syndromes of all kinds.

        After this tirade   I will walk rush run to the light
rail station and take the green light to teach for two hours and
deliver another rant   another tirade to my students about not

being the slave of the 21st century   all the while ranting and
all the while fussing   and all the while thinking about max
and annie sitting in the living room alone hungry and angry
                              I go on with my rant anyway
     As I tirade I would hear my cellphone trembling in my back
pack
here's the school leaving the message that my kids have not
checked in at their classroom in the morning
I know this already so do not call again or leave messages and
do not give me a call for each kids   theyre at home
Here I am making a fuss about standardizedhumanrobotized
and they are pissed off too for missing the bus
no   maybe they do not care at all   or maybe they are
in the living room with their backpacks over their shoulders
still and waiting and   watching Netflix a fair alternative
being late at the bus stop can bring on a Wednesday morning   I may have let the kids watch Netflix for
too long last night   it is maybe my fault they missed
the morning bus   We should have more rigorous bed time

     my laptop seems to think I owe him accountability and
     now I am returning to my previous sentence to turn the
word netfleas into Netflix thisisn't a mistake in my grammar of
things running   I proceed with a right click
     Add to dictionary
     the fairest thing to do though would be to put a zero and a
decimal at the beginning of a tag of an unwanted cloned sweet
potato marked $3 or more at a Cub or at a Target   How about
adjusting the clock's needles too
where was I?
     After teaching and ranting I would come back to the kids
          the way one comes back to time   as
if one could   take back
the lassitude the headache and the backache and the sighs and
the moans and the giving away cells blood and sweats and not
taking anything back
I can't   could not would not come back to myself
          And I would drop off the kids at their school very late
that Wednesday morning to leave the schools parking lot with a

big sigh in a big rush with other big things to do but

the nightmare I dreamed for so long finally came true
another item to check off in my to-do-list   with the
assumption that having missing the bus once or twice was
enough to get into the rhythm of not missing the bus anymore
during the quarter   of the semester   then I
would run to the food shelf pick up all the food that needs to
be picked up before   stopping at Aldi for the things
I would not find at the food shelf   the things I can't
pay for at Cub or at Target and even at Aldi the interstices a
small unwanted cloned sweet potato needs in order to
go rotting shrinking
in hell   very big

    Now
I cannot quite remember having told my students I have children   I will tell them this morning about Annie and
Max   to this I will add I can kick your ass I am not as young
as you think   I wont say anything   maybe I will   I
figured telling your students you have kids is something you do
in the beginning of a class   you present yourself you tell
them your background of all sorts who you are where you come
from and   you omit to tell them you eat at the food
shelf   this is isn't for them to know   what you
shit   where you shit
    I cross my fingers though
that being late at the bus stop never happens   at least not
on a Monday or a Wednesday my days of teaching and ranting
and confessing   the anxiety to not be late is a big thing
but should not   thereareno single roads to times I teach
my students
and this morning I will teach them to come back to time whenever they feel like it   the way you dispute a $3
rotten sweet potato at the open market   open time
        a kind of getting around

    I am sending the kids off to the bus stop handing backpack
coats water bottles and tying their boots and forcing them to
drink their morning lemon water   I run towards the

door that I open and hold for them to start running their way out
they're too slow
        they've run through the door already   I sigh I
shout I yell watch for cars when crossing the alley
                              It's my turn now
    I hope they won't miss the bus   I tie my shoes I put on
my coat and a hat
    I begin running very fast after them   I won't
catch them they are too fast running and I am already out of
breath walking very fast   in the middle of the alley
where they ran a few seconds before   The bus
had just left
    with them inside
even the tail of the yellow bus I do not see   but they're
inside so I figured that the chauffeur waited just a bit to not
leave them behind   a good thing after all that Max didn't go
brushing his teeth when I urged him to
            I sigh a big sigh   stand at the bus stop for
one minute or two   to breathe their outburst
the breeze they left on the sidewalk   I am sorry not
kissing you goodbyes

    I
really am   sorry   for all the pressures and the all
runnings and all the yellings
    It never occurred to me that the kids were at fault for
running all the time and for not sleeping enough and for not
having the room and the time they need to breathe and brush
their teeth   and put on deodorant and do their homework
with the best they could
    I figured it was the way to do things   to survive
moving abruptly from kids to teaching to grocery shopping to a
$3 sweet potato and taking it home for a few cents and moving
the kids after me as closely and as quickly as possible
And in the circle of running from one thing to another and
from one thing to another ceaselessly you give more than you
will ever take   you give too much   you give
what you don't have   always you continue giving yourself away
        and all the time you don't know all the things you are

giving up as you never stop with the running

    Still
I run back home quickly   things are the way they are   a
trap   I brush my teeth   put on some makeup
cover eye bags of 4 hours of sleep   I will not forget laptop
books and a banana to eat   On my way through the
door   I grab my coffee mug and my green leather jacket   My coffee mug is green   like a potato who doesn't
want to grow up   I rush toward the door
      In the green light train I am rehearsing my introduc-
tion for the morning class
I hope you are well this morning   and I need to check with
my friend later about this chiropractor who takes grad student
insurance   a chiropractor should be able to fix my neck and
my backache and my shoulders and my knees   I need to
run to Target at the end of the day to buy the melatonin for my
sleep problem I should sleep better tonight   maybe I should
just get laid   maybe I need more time to get more laid
maybe I should spend less time in front of the screen
there has to be a way to not let a curse get away with itself
and with me in passing

    In the classroom   I am
before a moving mass of faces   before a sea of
defiant eyes
you are looking at me   you're saying to yourself and at
the end of the session to your classmates   I am re-
dundant   repetitive   wordy   excessive
     and tiresome   I hope you are well this morning
and its boring   and I say it anyway   I forgot my green
coffee mug in the green light train   I am cold in my
green leather jacket   even my red hat I do not take off
before your green eyes
    My eyes are reddish and my shoulders falling   I have
sleep issues   I have hunger issues   I have
kids issues   and I don't have time to prepare
the teaching and   I don't need your
forgiveness

I had figured that with doing the best I can each day for
teaching   for kids caring
    and for staying alive   just to keep up with the running
each day each week with all the things to run after   if I shit
before your eyes   if I tremble before your faces   if I
am lost in myself all the time   I am still fine fine fine
doing the best I can   not that I lack the skills
to teach
that too I lack I shall confess   I must say with the lack
of sleep and with the lack of time plus the lack of food to eat
        one should not show up for teaching
Despite
    the class goes on so far so good
    a theater of the burlesque I am not even here   you're not
here in the classroom and you're not listening   and you're
not in the mood   and I am not in the mood
    All of you are running while sitting
    We're all in a state of suspension of passing in running
I pretend not to see you in your cellphone   matchcoming
tindering facebooking okcing expressionless   this is the
way of things   Now comes this student always late and
sleepy and bending   has he been drinking or partying
late last night or something   Maybe he has kids
        Maybe he has hunger issues   Maybe he ran
his last shift very late last night at a Target selling a $3 rotten
sweet potato root   I should cut him some slacks
leave him alone   or maybe not

    I am not a proper instructor
this   is the point of teaching you not to become slaves
don't you thinkI had assumed I should be more like an
exception   of a deviation of a defect   in search of eyeing
to turn itself into a possible norm and not wanting to go main-
stream more so for lacking the steadiness to fall then get up and
fall then get up again and fall again then get up again
    having more often not gotten up after falling and falling
and falling   Now I am not sure anymore how well I care about teaching and I even go thinking
you don't care either about learning   at least from me
you don't want me standing in front of you and ranting   but

we are all in this together   in suspension   authority
less   so far so good   not exceptionally   I hope
you're well this morning   I am by default

     doing well
     and always happy to be in the classroom
There is   in the teaching performance   a part that is steady
unshakable   unmovable
that moves round and around the cycle of a small potato root
for which you sometimes give $3 or $4 or more
and another part equally unchangeable   I tend to
forget   that   teaching is counter performing
you can walk into a store and leave on its shelves accumulated
          well-arranged rotten sweet potatoes   a skill I
had acquired over
     several years   the way
I walk out of the room
          I am a free woman Egg-in   one   less   day   of
teaching

     But a month ago it had begun wild   and promising
          I have the souvenir of having said something like

     I expect you to be fully present during your time in the
classroom   using any electronic devices will severely affect
your grade   class attendance and participation are
mandatory and will be documented
I didn't think I would get any close to dying like a root drying
up and fading   nor would you imagine a rotten
sweet potato getting in the way of
     giving the students a run for their money after the time that
always runs ahead

     Because   always time runs against you   and at
11:05 on a Wednesday morning   you figure
 time is a spirit threading through with their spiritual invisible
power pressing against you   despite a daughter conjuring over
a bedroom poster that says   never be in a hurry
And there are times I take back   you can return a

rotten cloned sweet   potato to itself too.

     At this time now   the kids are in recess or in the
cafeteria   They
    like the Wednesdays chicken patties   and the cheese
bread
Sometimes they bring me left over carrots muffins   I
like   from their
lunch cafeteria   I grab a cup of coffee at the office   go to the
    computer room   sit for a while to not see time passing
      through
there   I push the brain further and harder to manufacture some thoughts   on
    quitting being the slave I am   I teach what I am
    and I figure that   being surrounded with delusional hopes
and niceties and decorum all the while being pressed on
and against   I needed to sit through
time made spirit   cut through   and replace the
pressing order by my own senses of differential times
      whatever that might be   I don't know what it's like
    Therefore you cut through yourself
the way I left my breath in the coffee mug in the computer
room in the office   I hit the road to Aldi I will pick
up just a few vegetables and salads for a few days   I will to
go to the food shelf next Thursday   in my lucky day I find lots
of groceries and fresh produce for an entire week   not
even a rotten sweet potato root to be found

    I won I run I park my car in Aldi's parking lot   rush in
between a few aisles of the store   for the carrots the bacon
the buttered croissants   pay up the groceries that I
    carry on my hands on my arms   leave

I know for a fact you can walk into a store with no lists with no
bags get all the things you need   and walk out
    I will need to run quickly to TJ's now for the chicken fried
rice and the turkey meatballs the kid's favorite   a
quick solution to not having time for proper cooking or cook-

ing something Annie and Max will eat
The dream is to turn into a standard remoted human

have enough time to learn to make a grocery list
Still I would need to learn first how to work the plantation to
get food on the table   the kind of a $3 rotten sweet
potato you pick at your neighborhood handy Target
And maybe having enough time to not just run
but to wander between the isles of a Cub store   and follow
a recipe so we can stop eating TJ's   period.

it's almost time to pick the kids up at the bust stop now
what am I going to do
one should be given   even for once in their lifetime
the power to stop time
I cant   I rush towards Lexington Avenue   en route to
TJ's   I better not go after an accident   the kids
can wait at the door Beaude   its ok if you are late
its ok if they do not find you at the bus stop
and I listen to KTIS to stop my jumping nerves   I make it
safely to TJ's in less than ten minutes   at least they'll have a
good dinner   to   compensate my lateness
and I take the Ayr Mill road back   I command the bus   be
late   drive through Selby Avenue   all the traffic lights are
green
I get to the bus stop in less than 10 minutes
the kids are getting off the bus   I wave a grateful
goodbye   have a good evening to the bus
driver
leaving the bus stop

I miss waving you goodbyes this morning   I am sorry   it's
ok   they always say its ok
I will teach them its ok to say its not ok   to being
late at the bus stop   always and they're busy cartwheeling and jumping on the sidewalk s puddles
in between puddles jumping and cartwheeling   we have
turkey burgers for dinner
the sky is blue again   and tonight at 1:00 in the morning

I will refuse to do one
    more grading round   one more prep and sleep
six hours under
    rounds of night & night teas   I will pick up at
Target later   and
    fight being remotely driven and standardized and human-
ized
to stop one more black hair turning gray and keep fighting
being read on time or late or not proper
in my dream tonight
to hear something like the footsteps of my shadows my time

    You're the one going mad I am not late   nor on time nor
improper
    there are underneath my skin   cities   lovers
flows   flags   times   spices
    homes   waves   shits   truths
shapes   maps
    ghosts   pins   city lights   park benches desires
postcards   poems
    languages   forecasts   hungers   tomatoes
and broken lines and
    songs you cannot know
    if yall think you're on time or human or going 2020
go figure
    I am not the puppet   this time
        period

How are you?

You tossed it my way this morning, a name stitched onto a quilt,
it was your saying hello, and you continued walking your way not
meaning how I was doing, and I continued going my way not
caring whether or not you meant to know how I was doing, the
world goes on for you and me.

How are you?

    Oil smudging on water, and you mean it, at times to care, at
other times to romanticize my not being from here, my being
poor, my struggling, my not being able to make it, and then I

stop, I look at you beyond the bulk of your eyes, beyond the veil of your soul, and beyond your everything else.

How are you?
    You hear me, I say it right back at you, and I say it again, and I repeat myself very loud, and I stop everything else around, and I stop you in the course of your going on about your day. I mean it, and I really mean it, not that I care about how you are doing, but to remove from you the right you think you have over me to not being asked how-are-you back by me, poor thing.

The shared burden

The pleasure of going against analogical likenesses is a ride filled with stillness, with giving away white bones to the cold. Each jolt of the bus is dirt disturbed and deposited on a coffin, the manner I sit in the Greyhound bus on my going to my impediments. I am half dead in the chest gradually lowered into the bottom of the earth and pleasantly cold of a coldness not at all futile with the inconveniences leaving myself behind promises. I am thrilled.
    I get on the bus the way white blood cells work together, you shall not interfere. It's night; it's dark; it's rolling. I plunge myself into the underlayers of my hidden spots and sudden corners from *clé de fa* to *clé de sol* to being free of me. There's no destination but the stillness of having completed in all liberty a journey not yet known. Some rely on their body to bring them the *punto finale*. But what would become of me to not ride with all of my layers as to get rid of them? Being carried in spite and in-disgust amounts to walking towards the end with flesh and bones without getting there in soul, in spirit, and in everything else. I carry my chest box under my armpits, and my souls and my everything else rest in the palms of my hands. The blood in my veins heats my cells; I pour myself in from within; and my fingers are locked into a bulged fist throughout the ride, each night, five nights a week, each year. I ride the bus to downtown Chicago, to sell time; a parking lot attendant I am.
    And time I go sell, not because I have paid my debts, made my will, and settled my accounts or said goodbye to my lovers. I am not where my body is. To be frank, I am the powerless audience who cannot do anything about how fucked up the movie is. Nor

do I wish to maneuver my driver. I do not think I am a no-character in the movie. This betweenness is the focal point of life and death being incommensurably of equal value. Contemplating one's life going in disarray on a journey of no destination is uncontainable. You would learn to deal with it the way I do, dead and half dead, never wholly alive, nor fully dead. What would become of me not to walk with life under one foot and death under the other? Do not ask me how I have ridden myself out.

I went to say goodbye to my lover the other day; her body was already removed from me and from everything else; I found her belonging already cleaned up away. She is an absence. Let's say as if.

I breathe to hold the explosion inside my chest. I stomp my feet very loud. With each stomp the sound of my right foot hitting the bus floor competes with the noise of the running engine. What I would like to do is blow up, unleash myself against not being in accord with the objects of my beings at every turn. But all this seems extravagant. So, I keep my hands between my legs; my fingers are clenched; my shoulders are bent; my eyes drill the floor; the spirit of death filters in silence, within the slow rhythm of a *dorming* sea. I am not far from jumping over during the full seven hours of the trip, each second of the ride.

If you go to the troubled white man riding the bus, keep his breathing under your eyes, but remember to commence at your own door. Should I say, I am the fellow? Yet, do not fancy yourself with unnecessary associations.

From the people's etymology: white, seizure, morally bent, ethically fictitious, who get their living through conquest and rides. This tells you the kind of villainy I am liable to. But a half-dead man will stomp his feet once in a while against the coffin's cover for a discharge. A mortcloth will leave him indifferent. I am trying to tell you how betrayed I feel spitting my blood away in order to let live. A coffin will wrap its arms around you like the narcissist fiancé knitting a web of illusion around their prey or like the clock whose ticking makes you think you are the reservoir of infinity. You are not, I am not. Not all of us travel in prepaid roads. Besides, haven't you told me it's more than just locking my hair like yours in Bantu knots or the clothes; and there's the land, too.

I was served by the shawled woman at the bank last Friday. I could not look straight, a proof that infinity holds me. The driver of the big blue bus is blackly shaded. There is no limit to the kind of malice giving oneself the title of the ruler of the free world will engineer or of being whitened above everything else. I don't know any more if my salvation is to curse the shawl or the coffin weighing heavy on my neck. It's easy to curse a veil who seems to have taken my place behind the desk or the brown-skinned CEO who gets their sleep each night. I go for what I see. The hands of the clock turning is not the time. Nor is the ticking. In another life I feed my kids and send my wife to the salon each weekend without giving away my sleep. May those who has not sinned cast the first stone. I am not saying I have not voluntarily dispossessed my neighbor. Assimilation.

Then for a moment my palms rest on my chest. I sink in my dream. The dream of this other life in which I put my kids to sleep, and make love to my wife before I snore myself out. This is the dream in which I am the CEO or the banker or a driver, not a parking lot attendant who rides the bus four times a week. But a dream doesn't last, and you know that. I lie on my back in my chest. The cold splits my lips into dry purple stripes. I am cold. Who is my wife seeing tonight, how else would she take care of herself? We all do, take care of ourselves. I flee before her eyes to flee before my own eyes and yours, until the moment things crack up within my head. I will never be as good a man again.

The thing to do is to eye the woods within, the foot trails on the blue river that you name blackness or whiteness or aboriginal. The ride I wish to speak for, my own, the wilderness within where the world seems richer, wider, that I eye from this coffin, is untamable. This ride maybe you know, and on which some walk while others bus or take the highways or fly. Whether or not some of us are beneficiaries under some kind of treaty is something worth pondering over, don't you think?

Does my pinkiness cancel out my ability to travel with you in good faith? I don't think so. You do. My spirit rises above the swelling ocean, above the howling wind, and above the dense beds of shrubs rebelling against the botanist's enlightened hands, against the dubious zeal of the preacher's wife, and the boredom of the lawmaker, and against your hate and your anger, to return to where it belongs: the absent line between être and *ne pas être*, the wilderness that knows no laws but absolute idleness; the ride that binds us before definitions and etymologies and history enter the scene; the cracks that make me angel and demon, generous and greedy, black and white, and everything else you do not see, and bring me death and life on the same tray.

On this ground, in this ride, my wilderness throughout, my rage escalates and my heartbeats gallop. I breathe to preserve it against erosion, numbness, against the softness of all thoughts, and my fingers close the coffin lid over my nose to eye myself within as an enslaved privileged, and to know that something to do about being a half-dead man is to learn to be a parcel in the wilderness. There's nothing else.

The dream

In your pursuit of betterment
the dream
will hunt from faraway
to leave the shack the clouds
the kindred
for the land of the
(it can begin with the Sioux and the Mayas and the Aztecs)
free
the way I heard there was a dream

I knew no one who lived the dream
except for a farmer
who quits his pigs his chickens his cows and blueberries hills
to dedicate himself to more honorable thriving
a villa of a million chambers sitting on the mountain top
he saw then
into the back of a trailer in a community courtyard
he befalls to dream
the way of the traveler walking out of the backyard
(not that you shouldn't go after the dream)
nor that I have been concealing anything like learning the hows of
making something of myself

if I work hard hard hard
comply with god and the police lice lice
I will eat grass grass grass and chew chew chew
the land is possible and everything else
so very hard and fast I run
I walk
in the footsteps of the Latina neighbor
who catches naps in between shifts
and died beyond her steering wheel
or the forty-something husband
who promised to his wife their vacation dream
on faraway land (that might have been his
a century ago or so) then
in the middle of the night on his sofa
he passed
away after an 18-hour
shift to miss the next

the way I heard there was a dream
not that there is a word for the weight of running to catch up
with
with
bodies lawning the Roselawn cemetery
still
my friends and I plan a July 4th barbecue in Saint Paul's hot
summer
to celebrate indigenous land giveaways
still lawning and still running myself away
I will bring chairs made in Youwèsey dungeons for a few cents
a day
eat tacos from Mexico
and drink water from China
and settle a bit more in the familiar tangential
(not that I mean to pitch my tents into the land)
I knew no one who knew someone who lived
the dream

the way you heard there was a dream
from the floor of a basement made in Indonesia

(that everyone can make it)
except that the skins and blood of many dreamers would stretch
further than they can handle
exceed their dreaming capacity
and the feeling of relief at this stage of the journey you feel
before you can catch up with old selves you realize
the dream is the way of tonton sam of
blood coating asphalts and floors
at the sound of the police roars
and roars of Dontre Hamilton
of Philando Castile Eric Garner John Crawford Michael Brown
Ezell Ford Dante Parker
And Tanisha
Tanisha Anderson and Tamir Rice
Dreams made in Sandra Bland's blood of Yvonne Hakim Rimpel
and the chokehold of millions and millions more
coating asphalts and floors
and enmeshed with the smell of vaginaspussiesdicksandevery-
thingelse
taking over MN State Capitol
Rue du Champ de Mars and chanting
I am not for grabbing

and there isn't a way to say you're a slave or you're already dead
and already choking
and coating and lawning
something you could have been what you were
for the dream
is of the height of the Berlin wall
and as tiny as the hands of a people the soul
you can't see and
who panics over losing wars and battles and
to finish
the route you make backward
the moment they lost themselves
as you stand in your moment you feel
moving away from you
to return to
the land

the people the dreams of centuries ago
to come

MaxandAnn

The things that happened to time
A thousand years slipped through its threshold in a heated second
each day moving back and forth and back and forth
like in a tv moment of a commercial release

when the girl came out
she wore her hair half blue half yellow and
her eyes like a big cat
eyeing
a lightning rod

the boy came with
Darth Vader on his face fading
a faraway light coming
out of his right hand
there was the fire returning
and returning a different light
for a different balm of time to calm down

but like an electrical charge
out of his cape comes boredom
so suddenly
so obviously not flame nor fire
nor light inside but
unmoving times, panic attacks, and slopes:
like they all were made of fire of wires
of codes of kerosene inside .

the river is too muddy
I am allergic to trees
no biking let's take the car
google it
faster and
vlan and vlan and vlan
reminding me of the slowness of my mother

of my madness and compulsion for
darkness is all there is
then time keep burning itself out like
a light bulb remotely turned on and off
and on and off

but this is the new age
for all go nonstop like uninterrupted light bulbs
we will have a sleepover and
watch Logan Paul all night then wake up and
cereals and milks and banana muffins, school bus, snapchat, video games, pizzas, Logan Paul, sleepover then wake up and cereals and milks and banana muffins, school bus, snapchat, video
games, pizzas, Logan Paul, sleepover then wake up
leaving time numb and numberless
incapable of following its thread
now unattainable constellations
for maligned souls screeching out darkness inside
and I?
I just want to pat time's back
tell him it'll be alright.

I want to be hysterical the girl says and
teach history lessons about Ohio Fried Chicken and
a strand of orange is added to the hair turning
part blue and part yellow and part light
colorly fading to the point of
times losing reason
but what for?
time to spend time with my X-wing
the boy says
can we buy a fidget spinner?
I am anxious
fidget spinner makes you poop faster
google it
Ah if only you could see the inside out of light reded-blood wires
darkness-like on its other side.

so

home they go
with the hair a third blue a third yellow a third orange
and the air not so good
I am bored and itchy
and allergic to cotton God!
do not say god she says
say gosh
or fudge!
just the letter F but
you may say shshshshshshhhhh
ugar
and how do you say light saber in French
time is so identical to himself now on all points despite all your
saying
I bought a Lamborgini yesterday
for five dollars
have a castle on Roblox
and the boy gets louder with his sabre de la vie
that I took all in stride and personal
from not eating to going vegan and allergic and
machine like
in a kind of half-conscious lethargy

and all the many years of fists and rage and love
can't live in the same space as you
don't have any friends
cannot take away my phone
you need to do a musically with me
a comedy one then a song one
sometimes I wish
you're not the boss of me
'm calling the police
child abuse
can't sleep
can you pray for my nightmares
google it google it
I hate you
I wish
I am a youtuber

when I grow up
I don't like you
No w
I love you
can't you see
time standing still

I cannot say I am not amazed by the biosphere trimming itself
from plant to cotton grass to the frequency of faults within the
earth's crusts to molecules in symmetry.

So

You say you are Puerto Rican
not Mexican or Dominican or Brazilian
you have degrees live in suburbs pay taxes don't have a dozen
bambinos
not to mistake you for other Spaniards
you don't do parades you say
are too busy studying
and defending Youwèsey in every Youwèse war
each day being your war
see if your light accent is rolling you an ounce lighter in your
everyday war.

So you say you're not a freeloader
don't do food shelf
food stamp
you're not a *sanpapye* you say
you speak with a Brit-ish accent
come from the Haitian elite
and work hard for the American dream
to send *monegram* that get trapped into the traffic jam of memory lanes
how you burn yourself down like a circuit panel explosion out of
novel accents crossing

Don't you also say all the natives are dead
they come from India
and belong to Canada or Iceland

what else did you say
they're the worst kind of illegal refugees
who should be deported where they belong
the equal spectacle of wires crossing
of your breaking off into tiny pieces in all unresolvable directions
and unable to glue back
an unwanted world

What the heck
have we gone mad
I want to say
I say nothing
no-thing to say
when you consider that
after discharging your intimacy in your out-of-the-way remainder
room
you get up soldierly away from the shame below
away from the waste behind
already flushing it all away

none of this is me anymore.

Sans-nom

I don't know the name of my mother's mother. I don't the name of
my mother's mother's mother. I once asked my mother, over the
phone, about the names of her mother and her grandmother. In
this faraway conversation of checking in—how are you—where
is grandpa—Max and Annie are growing tall—I could sense her
fingers squeezing the phone's handle and her heartbeat racing.
She may have also pulled up a chair to support her shaking legs,
she must have wrinkled her cheeks, "but Beaude you've never
asked me those questions before" I heard her moan. I am writing a story about our family; this sounded like a confession; and
she paused for a moment; I could hear her laughing a little. The
sound of it was sharp and joyous and light, a sign she was sur-
prised. I have probably made her day by churning out her insides
and telling her how important the names of her mom and her
grandmother were. I hated myself for opening those suitcases

only in my thirties and a thousand miles away. Her mom's name was Retina.

I am the daughter of Mariette; the daughter of Retina. Mother does not remember the name of her mother's mother's mother, and in the early nineties all married women were Man. Man Echou, she said, and she moaned again. Her grandma took the name of the man she married and became Man Echou. She also said, as she continues moaning and sighing, it was a long time ago. I could hear her breathing through the phone, like each time a sigh decamps from her chest. She must have thought in all those moments of sighing and moaning about the cheery girl she was before marrying my father or how she has learnt to stuff up her voice, her name, her sighs between her shoulders.

I am the daughter of Mariette, the daughter of Retina, the daughter of Man Echou, and we ramble for a good five minutes. I meant to ask her about her nickname when she was a kid; I wanted her to babble the dreams she dreamt, the men she loved, the places she left behind, her selves wrapped up, buried. My father's sighs are well-crafted rolls of melodious thunder. We know who he is, what he likes, and what he is capable of by how he sighs. We know his name and the name of his grandpas and we didn't ask. My mom's voice has sometimes escaped after the shoulders were weighed down for too long. The name of the Man she carries is not her own.

And I turn off the computer. It's not knowing her story that brings long and ponderous sighs between my shoulders. Sigh. My mothers and grandmothers have been carried out of the field. Moan. I will not ask her if she's afraid her grandchildren won't remember her name. I will not tell her that Annie and Max know all my internet passwords contain m-a-r-i-e-t-t-e. We sigh and say goodbye, and I picture her murmurings and sighs and the echoes of her name rolling and moaning against the air, the water, all the names before her and the ground that tie us together.

Apparently

the courier could not deliver
no way
he could have stretched himself steady, integral, wholly untouched
without giving away by accident or fate or by impossibilities

himself or the word
or the world breaking loose with no intent
of terminus

no particular word to describe the thread
between two eyes eyeing and spacing
each other
the interstices that go unnoticed
erased from your memory lanes the second it comes into being
the this is it moment
Then you return your spit to your stomach
nothing for reason to cling on
giving yourself to a different order of things like
two cheeks of the face skewing each other out

and there's not a particular word or expression to birth for
the slit second that parallels
slightly almost
the gunshot
the quakes the crumbling the fall
the just just just right before
the raid the fire the war
when it strikes you with a ghostly speed
in the half of a half of half of a second
that makes life death's look alike
you will not return home for hot breads and chocolate

you would have to tell me
if there's an adjective a way to tell
his nose shaking in
your face you see behind his crust
and behind your pupils
his carving pain   on your face
that you are not even begging for it for
another day
to wink at you
after not winking

a name for that interstices

before it all blows up
did the rifle slip from his fingers for a second?
maybe yourself you felt already dirt
maybe at lost you felt to capture what life was about
a nothingness after all?
before your eyes the sensation of dying in
having never been
in your body stolen
enough to drive you into
a bliss under the rubble closing your eyes for
a different return
of things
of you

it is highly remarkable to seek to preserve the integer of time
and get it across while not losing its algorithms, its weight, its
breaking apart
in the middle of a delivery
sometimes
with excessive impressiveness
other times with shallow simplitudes
and losing all things
moment and touches and vision
in continuance

despite
you would have to tell me
how the world
says your name
the wind trimming your palms
your knuckles cracking
the sound of
your tornadoes
their impossibilities you would have to tell

Leaving self

Despite uninterrupted cracks and breaking downs, you enter the
stage all the time all wrapped up in yourself. You pick up and hold
up the world with a pervasive sense of palpability like a prisoner

with a full view of time in her narrow cell. Then the discomfort that pours down and stirs up from within for having stumbled upon a presence, a sigh, a light, a coma for which you are never too much prepared. This guilt I must live with I must confess.

You would notice the cellphone hiding under the veil of the woman holding herself behind her steering wheel; blame your friend Juanita who rekindles her ménage with her abusive white boyfriend; the child you judge talks too much and too fast you would redress. Then unexpectedly, a crack, a blow, an aperture from nowhere would help you catch yourself up after having drifted for too long and too deep and too settled. The life you wish sound, ongoing, and steady would crack up with much violence, a reminder of pre-established associations, of open worlds, slits, and your own trap you've laid.

And there is the way in which you distance yourself from those they tag sans-papier, undocumented, numberless, memberless who could be deported anytime; those with no recognition, who do not exist, are in transit; many who have stopped tracking times, geography lines, and nights from day and of whom you feel you're somewhat ahead of. In your blindness, you have become careless, untroubled, indifferent. I would turn myself toward the peep-hole, so many eyes watching back.

You have also supposed that we are what we eat. Self-preservation will bring ease, comfort, and a false sense of balance, especially when the power of blowing things up is stolen from you. You persist in your peep-hole, learn to keep the calculable *quant à moi* separate from the ramen noodle-addicted eater or from the all-day soft drink drinker. You are confined in a dual relation, you on one side and in front of you the eyes and the signs against which you try to repress any sorts of familiarity. You resolve yourself into having the whole wide world to stand against. It's so easy to love thyself. It's so easy to point at you. I would pity those who eat McDonald's at breakfast, lunch, and dinner and joke that they are a group apart who walks alike and talks alike and thinks alike. In truth, there is a maze of us.

At this point, you don't know any more to whom you owe allegiance. You make it a personal matter to insulate yourself from every day cares, confined you are in the emptiness of resilient self-sufficiency. And the game of lost-and-found you play with yourself. And the millions of times your selves flew away to never return back to you. Still, this is not enough for self-elevation and martyrdom. Then against the peep-hole you press again. I would look down upon those who shop at Walmart or Target and spit bitterly, we are not going to support modern-day slavery; this kind of bittersweet bitterness will keep your ego alive just enough to notice at times some correspondence between your selves and the objects of your voyeurism. The eyes that were there all along. You would continue to notice the young black woman carrying several young kids in her strollers, and talk of the Youwès citizens as a whole bunch of arrogant brats who put their noses where they don't belong and who should mind their own shit before going into the world to mend others' shit. I would peep, judge, stalk, assess, umpire.

One day, it all stopped all of a sudden. Maybe it was that I suddenly realized god-eyed-views peeping back, that I was living my selves from within and from out to the point both my outside and inward have become interchangeably the same, something neither you nor I but colored in you and me. Maybe it was when I understood that you do the things you hate with kernels of heartache for daily ratio, or maybe it is that I am both, the voyeur and the object of my pleasure. Maybe it was when I notice the turtle outgrowing its shell to strip away the veil that stands before its eyes but through which the religious man, the police, and the defender of civilization and myself make a living. It's more than that. It's more than that.

There was the moment you noticed the black couple struggling to sell homemade soaps under corporate threats, and another when you realized that both the Haitian and the American tailors are robbed by their own governments and corporate businesses. Now that we've blinked, we are also obliged to remember how all the father tongues mortgaged themselves out. Do you remember? Both of us where there each time my six-years-old son clenches my fists and hides behind my back each time he sees a police car. Now I must tell you the moment I joined my fellows in the land of unfamiliarity, unsettledness, and memberless to become sans papier, undocumented, numberless, in transit, and less than. We are emptied of even ourselves. Remember November 9, 2016? You cried out your guts that morning that for the first time you saw yourself as an American who did not deserve this shit and this shit and this shit.

This other time and all the times before when I finally understood all that was given, all the food I did not work for, all the life I did not fill in, that there are as many Youwès geographies, constitutions, and flags as there are American people. This other time you suddenly got better realizing that you live in a permanent nakedness, that anytime and anywhere you are a dead body, a stranger, an ungrateful rat whose passing and coming has no more weight than the bushes who give themselves in the morning to the water's repose then bow out in the blink of an eye before anyone notices that they've ever been there. In our blinkness, we must remember all the moments, all the beauties of us, and all the times we opened up ourselves before each other in our confine worlds.

To arrive at you and me, to see who I am and how I am in you and what you are in me, I must do violence against my selves and, with more indulgence, I must move along everything and everyone else. I shall undo my selves and go on leaving all of me behind, so that I may see beyond my flamboyant nose and roam through the fields, the hills, and the wilderness, free from references, malls, offices, and other worldly engagements. That's the real story, to tremble along the patterns of your journey and create communities with you and against you for a place where the world is so much more and so anew, and to say no, to stay mad, and to desire the sun in the depth of my bones and receive the sound of rain beads on my foreheads without frowning.

Ooooh this prison to each other we are where the gap between you and me is so evident and so false. I am sorry for all the times I peed, sneaked, judged, and pitied the great human adventure. You remain glue in me.

I am the disease.

For what do I know? What do I see other than all the things you mirror back to me, my derangement, my fear, my worlds, my inadequacies, and the everyday breakdowns and collages that never piece themselves back? How about the words I am so full of all the while they are so insufficient, so petty, and so about something else; all the while all the time they leave me hanging, unsatisfied, enraged. Can't you see?

What I see when I am full is always different than what I see when I am hungry and what you and I know together vanishes as soon as we depart from each other to be into something else, another friendship, another meal, another world, another word, another not necessarily better, but new, so better somehow. A new aperture always returns you to your peep-hole, your world, your word. So that, hungry or full I only notice in the passing encounter with hunger or joy or depression or thirst or love or you or the river pitching my name back to me. What is, remains a fleeting moment of a common performance of you and I. I am a piece of you, together on stage. That way only, with you inside, I can peacefully and serenely hate all the things I am and say to myself, we understand each other right from the start.

I shall admit that when I walk away in the moment of crossing, I bring you with me. I chew over you, over your lines, your energies, your sweat, our moment deposited in me. I am in love that's all. Like the other day, we were driving to church and my daughter got in the car to declare, as if coming to a sudden realization, you know what, it costs to be alive. I said yes, you're right, some of us do not deserve to be alive, we can't pay the cost. That's all I said, but I went on in my head searching for bliss and chewing, chewing, chewing, it costs to be alive.

You are a piece of me. I am a part of you. A part of the things I seek to understand, and the thing I seek to understand is constantly changing and changing me in the process of us seeking to know each other and understand. But there is this certitude: I know nothing without you granting me a presence. For that I am grateful for all the time you walked with me, assuaged my thirst, and brought me satiety and hunger, misery and bliss, hope and desperation, humanity and inhumanity and all the impossibilities that give me hold. I write with you, always, in that solidarity of vision.

And being a part of each other could be that, I am now apologizing for everything written here. I don't want you to love me any less. Even with you being my sustenance, I am a distorted witness. I talk out of desperation that I got to have that conversation. So many times, we sould have talked longer or clashed or poked at each other and get mad, and we didn't; we left things unsaid, thrown to angry winds. But I must borrow from Saint-Exupéry, *on ne voit qu'avec le Coeur.* The words out of which I attempt to sense and see, and feel are just treacherous; they are so disjointed, so untrue, and so not about you and I. What we said, lived, and did are untouchable. It must be that we remain in translation as my friend Richa would say. For, I do not even speak your language. And all the things I invent and imagine to justify and explain myself better so that some parts of me can indulge the whole me and understand why I write in a language that is not me, why you read in a language that is not my home, and the im/possibilities of all that . . . that I am all the time in the wrong.

I take consolation in the idea that I am not alone.

The only thing I am able to bring with me always is you. You give me sense of space. In you I find a solidarity of vision. How can I refuse your gaze upon me?

Of course, I read the great. Translation: I read mostly those that were available to me; and translating that: they were the most written about in the New York Times and whose writings I could find in abundance through a google search; a more correct translation: they're written in English and I could easily find copies from the library or buy them for cheap on Amazon or half. com; another translation not to lose: they were touchable. Not that I would not like to read Yannick Lahens' last novel or an essay by Marie Ludie Monfort. There was a language and its apparatuses that contained me and I wanted to be contained, at least for a while. I read Jamaica Kincaid, Phillip Lopate, June Jordan, Tony Hoagland, Gwendolyn Brooks. How I love Brian Doyle's Mink River! There was Trouillot's *La belle Amour Humaine* my friend Marjorie sent me from Paris I did not read. *There was Pluie et Vent Sur Télumée Miracle* I read so so long time ago to get to *The Bridge Beyond.* I read Natalie Goldberg's *Writing the Bones.* I read Karen Barad. I read Mimerose Beaubrun in translation; I taught Nagar's *Playing With Fire.* And Jigna brought me coffee at Surdyk's. I was also listening to Tracy chapman all day and all the time Freddie's "Time Waits for No One." I reached for a copy of Trouillot's *Le Bleu de L'île* to get instead *Le Petit Prince* and get it over and over in multiple languages and formats to love it even more. There were the times I reached for a friend's email to get her death instead. You always give something away, even the parts you don't know about, untouchable, distant, faraway parts. I owe that much to the touchable.

But you, you are me to me; parts and movements that remain distant from my grasp despite my working bones, blood, and words the way you work a land; sometimes raking, sometimes plowing, sometimes watering, other times waiting or standing by, and at times harvesting, but all the times dying. Because pieces of you vanish in the crossing. Because I am the piece of you that do not come back. Because you are those parts of me that return to me. You are untouchable. And you stand by long enough to witness that being is dying, there's always a price to be paid. The vanishing stays with you and bring you the sigh out of which you nail down a line of life in the movement of crossing; then you get a short-lived victory; then you have to reach again and again and again; you shall never rest. In this space where the imaginary meets the visible, where the touchable meets the untouchable, a bliss might offer itself to you after all, two or three centuries from now; ooh the stretches and the impossibilities of you out of which you write.

Or let's say I give you a piece of chocolate or a box of peppermint tea (it takes a huge amount of chocolates and tea to stir up things within you); or let's say your kids were very hungry, which says that you, not only, are hungry, but enraged and powerless and mad and suicidal and desperate and not human; let say you leave your house to go eat the sun and drink the cold outside your door, then you return home to find a bag of grocery lying in your living room because your friend sensed that the kids or yourself may need something to eat; or your friends bringing you to lunch and forbidding you from paying your share, and entertaining you to ease the uprooting, the anxiety, the madness; and again, let's say your friend takes the kids away from you for a weekend or for a week so you don't see yourself roaming the streets naked in the middle of the night all of a sudden; how about your kids not at all blind by your derangement asking you if you need a hug; or a faraway sister calling you to have you speak to your mother to ease your immigrant anxiety; all of their reaching out to parallel the homelessness, and homing you and teaching you that writing is living. These untouchables don't show themselves in a poem or a book for you to read but bring you lines of life that are as powerful as the lines of Tony Hoagland's Lucky.

It was during the season we saw the people elected a president with no birth place, no land, no body and whose language they were going to learn to speak; the season we walked several miles a day to catch up with our spirits and ate a lot of *tonmtonm* all day to get our memories back. One is so awake at home no matter what home tastes like on others' taste buds. Yet it was the season we learned home is a no place; the season the mothers hinted so you have found other mothers? But there were no other mothers to be found; the season we saw the dead falling and piling on top of each other like ducks mount their shit log on the edges of the lakes marking their territories; the season the suicidal finally understand that the living doesn't really care about a life gone, but only the shame of an empty life. As a refugee, an immigrant, an undocumented, a TPS holder, an alien on stolen land dying in slow motion, fully knowing they are dying, patiently witnessing the plunge, and eagerly making the descent, I hold on to a humanity reinstated and held by you. This, is another kind of translation, another way of being into each other. I owe that much to you. To you my family, my Lakou Annie Max Jade Marie Lily Cerat Pat and Steve Harlan-Marks Karen Sawyer-Smith Rosanne Zaidenweber Shawnya Haillin Johannah Hallin Leslie Myles Richa Nagar Zenzele Isoke Jigna Desai Kari Pederson and Kari Salmoski Nataša Ďurovičová Joelle Vitiello Chris Merill Karen Sawyer Smith Erica Berry Haley Konitshek Harriett Levin Milan Guerda Guerda Benjamin Francisque Naomi Scheman Marie Carmelle Omega Pierre Louis Eslie Jude Piquant Leslie Myles Emmanuella Norgues Vailola Monfiston Sherley Cooney Baudelaire Rosanne Zaidenwebe Anne adabra Barbara Youta Maelle Jesula Prophete Densie Axel Jade Marie Ludie Monfort Josie Clement Marjorie Maignan Laurel TU Kari Kari Pederson Smalkoski Marissa Hill-Dongre Denn Baudelaire Murielle Murielle Leconte Jean-Baptiste Madou Marie Lily Cérat Clément Benoit II Mariette Necker Sara Daniella Josie Martine Naimah Caitlin SeungGyeong Ji Chelsea Flaherty Hale Matshou Maija Colin Nayt Rundquist Travis Dolence Kevin Carollo Sam

Schroeder kim Todd Gaëtan Hartmann Tara Kennedy Madisen Anderson. You have given me, to borrow from my friend Pat, a scholarship to life. Now enough dying, enough rambling! Haven't you heard?

The Trial

don't go tell
the absence

she's of algorithms of
dots and genes not yet declared of

planets
in suspension and
not-yet-human
walking sticks

what is it to be
if not to
be an illusion

we've filled the blank page the silence
to overflowing
the possibility of absent silences that

I have supposed
it doesn't feel good to lose control to
not speak the language
Perhaps I should empty myself of all sensibilities
of all chatters all thoughts

Adding to that
what is gained from replacing the symmetry of emptiness
with the emptiness of symmetry?

*

Here, barbarous, insolent silence!

how long did the silence descend into its pit
without a trial a story
orphan like

As if there are silences to occupy
still
what crime committed?

There's never a right moment to be told about
an unknown species risen up from the shore of the Untold Blue
River
some 80.5 million years ago

it is permissible to say
human like
overriding the precious human cargo
(civilization, language, time, all the times, sea levels, bipeds and
memory lanes)
it may have begun somewhere   else
or the year before that or the year before that other year before
that other year before that

it might be practical to move from finer scales to finer and finer
scales
and keep going for

the times when the world's various fecal matters used to be one
body of fungal shit
Fecal as in fay-shhol   not in the manner two matters
from oblique roads converge in a single line of fecal exchange.

I am not saying we close up the sea of making sense.

There are pieces of evidence that symbiotic linkage between sin-
gle-minded organisms are at the origin of the unknown species
coma-shaped like.

*

And the neighborhood fishermen—*je pense à pêcheurs* not the sinners
discover an ankle bone
that of a three-year-old boy that was
of a baby cow and before that
of a horse smashed up and chewed by the water.
Think of an open-air museum:
each member of the kingdom is
a single-held organism built up by the turn-of-the-century
machine à fabriquer l'homme
not human nor thing nor noise
but absences and before that
silences.

Along with the silence there was the darkness fading
the night hauling
and the leaving murmuring *I don't want to go* or not yet
out of
a not-so-segregated section of an orchestra
before the organism finds itself in the process of becoming a thing
having left vicious acrid red marks on moving seas
and circulating like mobile gene and
hanging out with a variety of others
single-held alike but not really
before reaching the point of being the thing in happening
not yet happened

as each undergoes some sort of ongoing symbiosis
out of themselves
unaware unaware
unaware

Then you get an instance of eruption
the earth keeping itself awake un-balanced
in and out of its axis
beneath and above millions of tiny organisms for whom the line
between who is who is undecidable.

A chewed ankle in the river is a tree trunk

period
naturally doing its duty.

Who would have thought that the unknown species survived
all sorts of human happenstances
roaming the earth
the years ships and boats and millions of other human-like creatures crossed the Atlantic.

Could we listen to alternate superpositions
account for the songs of a whale
the chatters of black wasps
or a chewed ankle
their fault-lines
like an ordinary line passing underneath Santiago, Miyako, Jacmel
and underneath the rugs of your living room
stitching and sowing and covering
lines extraordinary enough to turn each other into
an inhabitant of a faraway planet
before each other's eyes

not that there could be an appropriate moment to make a re-
make of the music of
the earth of some billion years ago
in release now
what justice given?

*

Faultline: unseen junctions
unfelt movements

How can you trust the Homeland or the church or the classroom
teacher
taking over and accounting for the lines of cockroaches and
termites
but there's no history there
as if you didn't notice
underneath your living room a chewed ankle is

a tree trunk spilling over your toes
invading under your carpet's living room and threading itself
its own iterations at the corner of your toenails
that you squiggle out of your memory
superimposing your mark
without even a trial

Then the day you see yourself going out of sight behind your back
distributing your selves into others
stitching maps and genetics and fungi music among other species
how can you be so settled and so blind

not necessarily a call to the smartest molecules to be arriving soon
and going about their business

utter silence

*

the century to come will never come soon enough
to wipe out the shit the vomit the cracks and the darkness
of yestercenturies

we heard
the 11-year-old girl saying
you are going to save the ant this time
This time was a halt in the pilgrimage of memes seeking symmetry with cells
and fingerprints and unknown stars turning
human faces above feeling stronger
because bigger
into a flashlight on the vacuum
I will this time the mom replies
The 11-year-old stares
joining up
coding up
and a node is vanished in the inseparability
of sound and silences
The ant was no longer one ant

and the little girl is counting one ant dragging a grain of rice
with a fellow ant pilgrim
two more three more four more
little girl counts
unaccountable moistures
carrying themselves through
the gallop of the horses
And the ants desperate to model put themselves out of their own
wings
The little girl who was no longer a little girl bends her knees and
her shoulders
her face is the ground in which she crawls after
after the ants who are now too many
and counting
everything is a bite and
relative and related and
chewed into each other
the little girl was no longer counting
you are going to save the colony
mother ant has her nest in my pillow
make no promise the mom says as
The ants continue their marching on giant columns of macaroni
and cheese
at this node they were already quite a crowd
rising like the faces above the ground
introducing geometrical deviations
throwing time into shades.

*

How long did the silence linger?

unlike a skeletal of
letters and lines stirring themselves up and
turning into prints
Unlike Moses standing on the mountain top with the great plates
sliding down
the land and in
a quake kind of movement launching God's armies into wars

opening up fault lines and seas and novel territories
and rearranging
bodies
subtracting lands, geography lines, and water holes
all of them
auditioning with minutiae
the standing of continents and human races
and ethnicity But
not at all accounting
some other plates and lines
smaller in size
covenants Brother Moses overlook from the top of the mountain
unlike the breath of the mountain
that preserves the imprints of waters on bushes
It felt strange posturing
the small
seeming weak in symmetry
the inside out of
A monarch sizing up at a distance the enfolding of things
the throat of the lands
and many other things from the ant to the cow
and from their colony journeys
centuries ago or so throughout El Karibe era

Before that there might have been
many more non-declared fogs and frogs and lights
before all that there was
a hearing
without the jury and
the victim was the accuser in a wilderness of
cows of sheep singing lullabies across
a continuous music of a thousand geographIES
Each line of the cow was a promise
to repair and mend and bring about
a chewed ankle
and a chewing water that will not turn itself into butter
as the cow parades

The sheep comes out of the bench

and won't make up his mind
or not yet
how many to tell how many to count
the day the gavel echoes
ain't that great ain't that great
a cow on a trial is a matter of translation
the civilization project is doomed
the rivers hear
the verdict
everything is everything else and relative
and related

just ask the ants
or the flies or
the fruit that flies and
the fruit flies
that come and go
each spring each summer
the fruits meet the sun
a fruits flies pops up
Ants are fruits flies
MosquitoESs are fruit and ants and flies
the stinky stingy big flies are fruit flies

The way fruit flies are gentle and pleasant and sufferable
the way fruit flies are of fruits
and not of locked dark carpeted rooms
cornered within rugs finely severely knitted within children
dogs and cats' juices and other sluggish things
or the toilet bowl that carries an air of grease
of thick yellow sap and other watery solutions
like spits and blood and pieces of fecal matters crushed up but
thickly holding on
hasta la victoria siempre
with rats on promenade and appealed by bags of meats,
leftopened diapers and rotten vegetables and fruits stuffed up
and turned into more grasses and cracks and saps in moldy
smelly kitchen garbage cans to which the smell of bed wetting of
dirty microwaves and refrigerator

set out to cook
all of that
winter and fall throughout
spring and summer too
until all of this gets out into unwanted cargo
A good translation to living in a shit-sea
is fruit flies taking over
behind locked heated doors

so much effort to not see the faces of thermites and
the likes thrown upon the turbulences and decays
our sense of decomposition
the continuous music in denial
a mushroom is a toadstool
period.

No explanations
to being made
of computer wires and lights
and granules
the way tiny organisms from the shore of the Untold Blue River
pursue their sympathetic symbiosis random living matter you sing
as if to single them out
the way of a granule in a sandbox
of a tiny organism setting out to conquer lands waters and bodies

Throughout history of the modern world no one has seen the
small creatures
a key reason:
the EYES that were watching back.

*

Ask grandma who owns three cardigans
a few never faded dresses
there is in her ancient drawer an old pullover that shrank to a
smaller size that
keeps getting smaller
and shrinker and immortal

just ask grandma's body crowded with convulsion
not for her accumulated years or
a pullover that goes on shrinking
There are monuments of accumulated moments droplets moistures and
and whispers and spits and tufts of hair that camp in grandma's
body closet
depositing all kind of matters
at the echoes of faraway songs
at the trembling of distant notes

fingerprints:
absences of that which unknown from
trails of accumulated pheromones
biometricizing
the sigh that is an en avant
in the movement backward inward
the sound of you
mutually not exclusively
pieces of many
the silence that walks before the cows in the morning parade
to wait for what will happen next
the delaying the disappearing reappearing before
the breaking apart
the fingers patching sowing assembling the pieces of fabric of
grandmas'
dresses and cardigans and sweat
and scraps from which all is measured
Here for the back and here to cover the chest and the feet and
this part for the legs
Here's for the head
and the world making of empty darkness
not to forget fungal fingers unearthing potatoes and sending
them to the morning tables
To your table across a thousand miles
and voyaging with their trails and their traces on behalf of
the absences of particles you bear
With no requests of adoption from you
but jumping around borderless

So you can pretend not to know who I am
industrialize my fingerprints my gene
and measure biometrics and blood
as if you were not my host
as if I wasn't yours
as if there were boundaries
between us
As if you could tell where your music originates
as if freedom was an equal trade-off

It is impossible to build a wall in the lines of
prokaryotic microorganisms
because all measurements remain and
their swerving is a form of re-
mapping you cannot see
disabling

*

To imagine the maze of accused and jury and witnesses as parades of infinite
sounds and waves and languages
clothed with silences
To see the trial trails itself from myriad corners of countless
world corners
the infinity of lines of thought after which we walk so that we
can no longer tell the path we walk on
the traces out of which we walk out
the way we've been doing the wondering through the vacuum
like forever like forever
forever
tuned to infinite landscapes, sound, nodes, points
and waves and traces
no matter how hard you try to shut yourself away or measure me up
The way of your bottoms rocking the ground
with the sun over your naked heads and
your knees and your years tangled up into themselves and into
each other
and we are young and they are old and

they are young and we are old and some of us less old or much less young and
others much older and younger and many more
untimely timeless and all of us naked naked
naked
slits and traces of all there exists

Plus the sound of hungry ashy feet hammering the ground; bodies chinned up by the million directed towards the sun trembling with fear and the sound of horses hooves opening up the cement and the millions more hooves shaking the hearth and its hearth in unison, advancing; and imagine all of us, all of there has been, more than can be counted and seen and imagined; and we sigh and we tell, we sing, we whack, we un-biometricize, we jump, we clap; imagine the sound of heavy, hungry, uneasy rice and beans hitting, stabbing the bottom of millions of cans like beads raining down clap clap cladap clap cladap clpacpalappclaccclapp.

The plea

The awakening of the people is a city of nobodies
of waves unleashed
no-one-can-say-no-bodies-is-not-real
or another knows too much or too little or speaks nonsense or is black or Mexican or red-skinned. There must be some kind of logic behind nobodies entering the city or rewriting the Alamo battle or not raising the flag
or saying no two words to languages and to passports
or taking down the walls and walking on red lights
or kneeling
to find ourselves in cities of waters
in quakes calling quakes
in lights and river lines
intermingling

A courtroom as wide as the sky
a dome made up of Seattle and Corinthians and St. Augustine engraved
in the misplacement of the 14th century postmarked

from the river
no longer capable of belonging to
the electron a little odd and a bit more
strange and
on their mission to hit a detector screen so they can somehow show
you are beyond being diseased and flawed
You breach your way through two narrow slits standing near
each other
and mingling
with other particles and agents and moistures not because some
of you travel together through one slit or the other— let's say
you speak the same language or walk the same land or are
covered by the same century blanket—-but you hang out and
touch and return over and over on yourself and with others and
on others through both slits simultaneously and through
indeterminate slits you make you don't know
to find yourself scattered and threaded
and thrown
laid in parts and in wholes and carrying several gang member-
ships you don't see
to turn inside out and upside down
the century era screen
you claim

Despite the indeterminacy
you insist in lines so settled and so straight
if I have adhd
if of the land I am a prisoner
if I am stamped already
or recognized
There is more to the city than its avenues
rivers and lights and atm machines and malls and
Despite ourselves we hold our foreheads as scanners to hear
through the silences out of which

the accuser is nowhere to
be seen.

About the Author

Beaudelaine Pierre is a journalist, scholar, and novelist who writes about her native Haiti and her adopted Youwès. The essay for which the present collection is named, "You May Have The Suitcase Now", is the winner of the 2019 CDS (Center for Documentary Studies) Documentary Essay Prize.

The author thanks Kim Todd, Karen Sawyer Smith, Erica berry, and Hale Konitshek, for their terrific support in the writing and revision of the essay "You May the Suitcase Now" included in this volume.

Other Works from the Author

Foufoune, Une soirée Haïtienne, Ed.Thomas C. Spear: Les Éditions du Cidihca. 2020

L'enfant qui voulait devenir président. L'Harmattan, 2012.

How to Write an Earthquake / Comment écrire et quoi écrire / Mò pou 12 janvye. Autumn Hill Books, 2012. (Co-edited with Nataša Ďurovičová)

La Négresse de Saint-Domingue. L'Harmattan. 2011.

Testaman. Port-au-Prince: Bon Nouvèl. 2003.

About New Rivers Press

New Rivers Press emerged from a drafty Massachusetts barn in winter 1968. Intent on publishing work by new and emerging poets, founder C.W. "Bill" Truesdale labored for weeks over an old Chandler & Price letterpress to publish three hundred fifty copies of Margaret Randall's collection *So Many Rooms Has a House but One Roof.* About four hundred titles later, New Rivers is now a nonprofit learning press, based since 2001 at Minnesota State University Moorhead. Charles Baxter, one of the first authors with New Rivers, calls the press "the hidden backbone of the Americ an literary tradition."

As a learning press, New Rivers guides student editors, designers, writers, and filmmakers through the various processes involved in selecting, editing, designing, publishing, and distributing literary books. in working, learning, and interning with New Rivers Press, students gain integral real-world knowledge that they bring with them into the publishing workforce at positions with publishers across the country, or to begin their own small presses and literary magazines.

Please visit newriverspress.com for more information.